TELLING GOD'S STORY

YEAR FOUR:
THE STORY OF GOD'S PEOPLE CONTINUES

INSTRUCTOR TEXT AND TEACHING GUIDE

TELLING GOD'S STORY
YEAR FOUR:
THE STORY OF GOD'S PEOPLE CONTINUES
INSTRUCTOR TEXT AND TEACHING GUIDE

RACHEL MARIE STONE

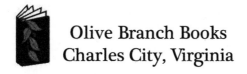

Olive Branch Books
Charles City, Virginia

For my children—
and for all of God's children.

Publisher's Cataloging-In-Publication Data
(Prepared by The Donohue Group, Inc.)

Names: Stone, Rachel Marie, 1981-
Title: Telling God's story. Year Four, The story of God's people continues : instructor text and teaching guide / Rachel Marie Stone.
Other Titles: Story of God's people continues
Description: Charles City, Virginia : Olive Branch Books, [2018] | Interest age level: 009-011. | Interest grade level: 3-5.
Identifiers: ISBN 9781945841309 | ISBN 9781945841316 (ebook)
Subjects: LCSH: Jesus Christ--Biography--Study and teaching (Primary) | Jesus Christ--Teachings--Study and teaching (Primary) | Jesus Christ--Miracles--Study and teaching (Primary) | Bible. Acts--Study and teaching (Primary) | Bible. Epistles--Study and teaching (Primary)
Classification: LCC BT207 .E56 2018 Year4 TchrMan (print) | LCC BT207 (ebook) | DDC 232--dc23

Table of Contents

Introduction   **9**

Unit 1: Jesus Departs—and God is Faithful

Lesson 1: Continuing Jesus' Story (Linking Luke-Acts)   14
Lesson 2: Gone but *not* Gone (Acts 1:9-14)   17
Lesson 3: What is an Apostle? (Acts 1)   21
Lesson 4: God's Deliverance: The Exodus, Jesus, and Evil
   (Acts 2:22-41)   25

Unit 2: The Holy Spirit

Lesson 5: Tongues of Flame—Babel Undone (Acts 2:1-21)   32
Lesson 6: Making All Things New: Times of Refreshing (Acts 3)   35
Lesson 7: Life in the Spirit (Galatians 5-6; and Romans 8)   38

Unit 3: The Cost of Following Jesus

Lesson 8: Persecution by Religious Authorities (Acts 4:1-31)   42
Lesson 9: Prison Doors Open (Acts 5:17-41)   45
Lesson 10: The Story of Stephen (Acts 6:1-8:3)   49
Lesson 11: Conflicts with the Culture and Setting All Kinds of
   Captives Free: Paul and Silas in Prison (Acts 16:16-40)   54
Lesson 12: How Can Trials Be a *Joy*? (James 1)   58

Unit 4: Being a New Creation in Christ

Lesson 13: An Outsider is Welcomed In (Acts 8:26-40)   61
Lesson 14: Being in Christ, Being a New Creation
   (2 Corinthians 5; and 1 Peter 1)   65

Unit 5: Who is Paul?

Lesson 15: From Enemy to Brother: The Conversion of Saul
(Acts 9:1-9)   69
Lesson 16: What Paul Gave Up (Philippians 3)   73
Lesson 17: Paul, the Idols, and the Philosophers (Acts 17)   76

Unit 6: The Good News is for Everyone!

Lesson 18: Peter Goes to Cornelius' House (Acts 10:1-48)   81
Lesson 19: What Do *Gentiles* Have to Do to Be Saved?
(Acts 15:1-35)   85
Lesson 20: Salvation by Faith (Romans 3:21-31; Romans 4)   89
Lesson 21: Essential Love (1 John 4:7-21)   92

Unit 7: The Life of the Church

Lesson 22: The Shared Life of Jesus' Followers (Acts 2:42-47;
4:32-37; 5:1-11; and 6:1-7)   96
Lesson 23: Sharing Different Gifts within the Community
(1 Corinthians 12; and Romans 12)   99
Lesson 24: Don't Be Divided: You Belong to Christ, and Christ,
to God (1 Corinthians)   103
Lesson 25: What is Faith—and Why Do We Suffer?   106
Lesson 26: Faith Must Express Itself in Works, Not Just Words
(James 2)   109

Unit 8: After Death

Lesson 27: Peter Heals Aeneas and Raises Tabitha
(Acts 9:32-43)   113
Lesson 28: Suffering, then Glory (Romans 8:18-39)   116
Lesson 29: Living Between the Times; Grieving,
but with Hope (1 Thessalonians)   119
Lesson 30: The Importance of the Resurrection
(1 Corinthians 15)   122

Unit 9: Last Things

Lesson 31: Christ, the Mighty Conquering One (Revelation 1,
    especially verses 12-20)   127
Lesson 32: God Makes All Things New (Revelation 21)   131
Lesson 33: Come, Lord Jesus (Revelation 22)   133

Unit 10: These Three Remain: Faith, Hope, and Love

Lesson 34: Faith (Hebrews 11:1; Galatians 5:6;
    Ephesians 2:8-10; and James 2:22)   138
Lesson 35: Hope (Romans 8:24-25; Romans 8:24-25;
    1 Peter 3:15; and Hebrews 11:1)   140
Lesson 36: The Greatest of these is Love (1 Corinthians 13:13;
    and 1 John 4:8-16)   142

Introduction

My first class in graduate school was Medieval English Drama. We studied the mystery plays—mostly those known to us today as the York Mystery Plays, which you can still see performed in some places throughout the world. For ordinary medieval people, many if not most of whom were largely illiterate, the mystery plays depicted the drama of humanity's life with God from Creation to the Last Judgment, and they depicted it with humor, reverence, and, sometimes, with astonishing insight. I was surprised by the unusual emphases and interpretations the plays offered.

It was astonishing, for example, to see that when God banished Adam and Eve from the Garden of Eden, he sent them to "middle-earth." What could that mean? Perhaps, some suggested, middle-earth is simply where medieval English people imagined themselves living: not below in hell, nor above in heaven, but in the middle, on the earth—middle-earth.

But perhaps, as well, Adam and Eve's expulsion to middle-earth signified something else in the imaginations of these medieval theater folk. For Adam and Eve, like us, live between the times—between the paradise of Eden and the joy of the New Jerusalem. Perhaps even the play depicting the banishment from the garden suggested a kind of mercy: the mercy of the creation of time where there had once been eternity. Rather than being eternally damned, Adam and Eve were given the mercy of time, in which God's redemption would be revealed.

This volume of *Telling God's Story* takes place in a similar sort of middle-earth. Jesus departs, but rather than signifying tragedy and the end of the story of God's life with God's people, it opens up another merciful window of time—time for the Gospel to spread throughout the earth, time for more people to be gathered into the family of God. And in this middle-earth setting, Jesus' followers are given the job of

9

extending Jesus' work—his teaching, his healing, the hope of his resurrection—throughout the earth, in anticipation of the time that is to come, when every tear is wiped away, and sorrow, tears, and death itself will be no more. The lessons in this book explore the mystery of living as Christians in the meantime—the in-between times.

A fuller explanation of the methods behind this program is found in the core text for this series, *Telling God's Story: A Parents' Guide to Teaching the Bible*.

Organization

The lessons for *Year Four* are centered on understanding the in-between times—what happens when Jesus leaves? How is his story continued? What does it mean to live in the way of Jesus? The lessons are organized into ten units, each covering an important aspect of the New Testament:

UNIT 1: Jesus Departs—and God is Faithful
UNIT 2: The Holy Spirit
UNIT 3: The Cost of Following Jesus
UNIT 4: Being a New Creation in Christ
UNIT 5: Who is Paul?
UNIT 6: The Good News is For Everyone!
UNIT 7: The Life of the Church
UNIT 8: After Death
UNIT 9: Last Things
UNIT 10: These Three Remain: Faith, Hope, and Love

Aim to complete one lesson per week. This book is designed to be used along with *Telling God's Story, Year Four Activity Book: Student Guide and Activity Pages*, (available for download at welltrainedmind. com) which contains pictures, projects, and other activities. You may wish to read the scripted lesson to the child on the first day as he or she colors the picture, and then complete projects on the second and third days. Alternately, you may read the scripted lesson on the first day, complete the coloring picture on the second, and complete a chosen project on the third. In a group setting that meets once a week, plan to read the scripted lesson as the students color and then to conclude the day's study with one of the projects or games especially designed for group use. You may find it helpful to both open *and* close your work with the scripted lessons, or to invite children to retell the story after they've heard it, perhaps using small figures or other manipulatives.

Each of these units comprises several lessons, which means that you will spend several weeks on each unit. The order is not unalterable, but neither is it random. We start with the story of Jesus' departure and end with his Second Coming; and the middle is all about how Jesus' followers did (and should) live in light of these two great events.

The first three units ("Jesus Departs—and God is Faithful," "The Holy Spirit," and "The Cost of Following Jesus") seek to form a link with *Telling God's Story, Year Three: The Unexpected Way*, even as the book of Acts is really part of a two-volume set—Luke-Acts. As Jesus departs, God's presence abides in the coming of the Holy Spirit, who begins to dwell in Jesus' followers, who continue his work—and face persecution because of their faithfulness.

The fourth unit, "Being a New Creation in Christ," along with the fifth and sixth, ("Who is Paul?" and "The Good News is for Everyone!") delve into the question of what it means to "be born again." Because Paul is the theologian of the early church who wrote extensively on this question, several lessons focus on the range of his teachings, including the important questions of "For whom is the Gospel?" and "What must one do to be saved?" The seventh unit addresses the related issues of the common life of the church: how Jesus' followers learned to share responsibilities and resources, and how to deal with conflict.

The next two units, "After Death" and "Last Things," explore, first, the centrality of Jesus' resurrection to the Christian faith and its relationship to Christian hope: What has the Christian to fear if Jesus has conquered death? "Last Things" introduces children to the often confounding book of Revelation, but instead of the Hollywood-inflected sci-fi version found in some interpretations, these lessons interpret Revelation as a return to the Garden of Eden, which is transformed into the City of God that fills the whole Earth, where, at last, God dwells among people and death and sin are conquered once and for all.

The final unit, "These Three Remain," concludes the course by helping students understand and cultivate the three essential virtues praised by Paul in I Corinthians 13 as "the things that remain forever": Faith, Hope, and Love. The three lessons in this unit explore these often-misunderstood virtues and encourage children toward a lifelong journey of practicing them.

Even though the order of the lessons is intentional, you should feel free to alter the order to suit your own purposes, particularly if you are seeking to link your lessons with the lectionary readings or the Church

Year more generally. "Lesson 5: Tongues of Flame—Babel Undone," for example, could stand alone on Pentecost.

Each lesson opens with a brief word of explanation to the parent or teaching adult. These are more detailed and complex than the scripted lessons to be read aloud; think of them as mini-commentaries. I've tried to include the major theological and critical questions that arise in each passage—not that these will necessarily be questions that the children will ask, but because they are things that I've found good to know; things that have deepened my reading of Scripture and my understanding of Jesus.

All scriptural excerpts are drawn from the New International Version.

Unit 1

Jesus Departs—and God is Faithful

Jesus' followers were devastated when he died: it seemed impossible to them that he could actually have been the Messiah, the Anointed One of God, and yet suffer a shameful, criminal's death.

But he rose from the dead, and he is alive. And that God's Messiah would suffer was not, from the point of view of the Hebrew Bible, at all unexpected.

Still, his followers were surprised, and then even more astonished when, just as they were hoping and expecting that Jesus would restore the kingdom to Israel and end their exile, Jesus didn't quite answer the question, instead charging them with being his witnesses in all the region—and all the world.

And then Jesus departed, leaving his very surprised followers to continue his work.

The lessons in this unit are a bridge from the work of Jesus in the Gospels to the continuation of his work by his apostles, through the help of the Holy Spirit.

Continuing Jesus' Story

What the Parent Should Know: In our Bible, the Gospel of John separates the Gospel of Luke and the Acts of the Apostles, but in fact, Luke and Acts form a literary unity; a single book traditionally understood to have been penned by a single author. Scholars often speak of them as such: "Luke-Acts." That they are two halves of one whole—"Volume One" and "Volume Two"—is clear from Acts' prologue:

> In my former book, Theophilus, I wrote about all that Jesus began to do and to teach until the day he was taken up to heaven, after giving instructions through the Holy Spirit to the apostles he had chosen. (1:1-2)

Why, then, are Luke and Acts separate? Perhaps they are separate because in the present canonical order, Acts forms a good introduction to Paul's letters, or perhaps because Acts is simply unique among New Testament books. Either way, it is clear from the superscription and from the character of the books themselves that Acts continues the story of Luke.

In the book of Acts, Luke is concerned to show how Jesus' story is rooted in Israel's story, and to show that God was not only faithful to his promises to Israel, but has also extended those promises and blessings to all people, including Gentiles (non-Jews). The apostolic teaching within the book draws deeply on the Old Testament, stressing that God's promise to Abraham in Genesis 12:2-3,

> I will make you into a great nation,
>   and I will bless you;
> I will make your name great,
>   and you will be a blessing
> I will bless those who bless you,
>   and whoever curses you I will curse;
> and all peoples on earth
>   will be blessed through you . . .

is now being fulfilled as the good news of Jesus is offered not only to Israel but also to all nations.

Commentators often note that the book of Acts follows a structure based on geography. As New Testament scholar Luke Timothy Johnson notes, Jesus' final appearance in Luke (24:47-49) sketches the outline of Acts: "Repentance for the forgiveness of sins will be preached in his name to all nations, beginning at Jerusalem. You are witnesses of these things. I am going to send you what my Father has promised; but stay in the city until you have been clothed with power from on high." Many readers observe that Jesus' words to his disciples at the beginning of Acts outline the book as well: "But you will receive power when the Holy Spirit comes on you; and you will be my witnesses in Jerusalem, and in all Judea and Samaria, and to the ends of the earth." (1:8)

Indeed, Acts follows this very structure. The first part of the book takes place in Jerusalem (Acts 1-7), followed by Judea and Samaria (Acts 8-12), and then Asia Minor and Europe (Acts 13-28). However, Jerusalem remains central in the story, with events in Jerusalem narrated all throughout the book. This is because Jerusalem is central to God's promises to Israel and, as the place of Jesus' crucifixion, to the birth of the church.

The book of Acts is often labeled "The Acts of The Apostles" and has also been called the Book of the Holy Spirit. The Holy Spirit is active within the book of Acts, guiding and driving the apostles' ministries; there are five separate accounts of the "outpouring" of the Holy Spirit within the book (2:1-4; 4:28-31; 8:15-17; 10:44; and 19:6), including the famous "tongues of fire" at Pentecost. The ministers of the Gospel in Acts are described as being "filled with the Holy Spirit" (4:8; 5:32; 6:3; 7:55; 11:24; and 13:9), and, as scholars such as Luke Timothy Johnson note, are portrayed as prophets among the people of Israel. They perform miraculous signs and wonders, as prophets do, and they preach and reveal a message from God that is met with significant opposition, as prophets do—Jesus and John the Baptist included.

Acts is also significant in that it narrates the continuing story of Jesus' work as carried on by the Holy Spirit in the church that is forming. The term "Christian" is coined in Acts, and it is in this book that Christians are first called "Christians" (11:26), and, emerging as a distinct group, become the targets of persecution. But, paradoxically, that persecution only seems to strengthen the movement, as if to affirm, as Jesus' death and resurrection affirmed, that suffering, even suffering unto death, can be redeemed for God's good purposes.

Begin by reading aloud:

Have you ever read a story or seen a movie that had more than one part? Many popular books, such as *The Lord of the Rings*, are broken into several parts. *The Lord of the Rings* has three parts, and is sometimes sold as three separate books, or *volumes*. But *The Lord of the Rings* is also sold as a single, very thick book, because it is really one single story. If you were to read them out of order, or to read one of them without the others, you would not be getting the whole story, but only part of it.

The book of Acts—which probably has the title *The Acts of the Apostles* in your Bible—is something like that. We can think of Acts as "Volume Two" of a single book called "Luke-Acts," because it continues the story begun in the Gospel according to Luke. (Acts doesn't actually come after Luke in your Bible for all sorts of reasons we won't get into here.) But the same person wrote both volumes, and Acts continues the same story that Luke's first book began. Here is how Luke introduces the book of Acts:

> In my former book, Theophilus, I wrote about all that Jesus began to do and to teach until the day he was taken up to heaven, after giving instructions through the Holy Spirit to the apostles he had chosen. (1:1-2)

So the book of Acts is "Volume Two" of the story about Jesus begun in the Gospel according to Luke. But what is interesting and even a little strange about Acts is that Jesus himself is only there for the very first part of the very first chapter, and then leaves. How can Acts be a continuation of the story about Jesus if Jesus isn't even there for most of it?

At the end of Luke's Gospel (which, you'll remember, is "Volume One" of a single book, Luke-Acts), Jesus tells his disciples to take his teaching "to all nations, beginning from Jerusalem." Jesus' story is "to be continued . . ." *by Jesus' followers*. As Jesus is leaving, at the very beginning of Acts "Volume Two," he says:

> . . . you will be my witnesses in Jerusalem, and in all Judea and Samaria, and to the ends of the earth. (1:8)

Do you know what a "witness" is? A witness is a person who sees something take place, and can testify—that is, tell other people—that it really happened. Jesus is asking his disciples to continue his work by *witnessing* what they have seen and what they have learned from Jesus.

And what have they seen? What have they learned? They have seen that Jesus is God's son, and that in Jesus God has kept all of his promises to his people. They have seen him teach that following God is not about keeping a set of rules but about loving God and God's people, especially people who are poor or excluded. And they have seen Jesus get into big trouble for this teaching. They have seen him be killed for it. But they also have seen God's power in raising Jesus from the dead—what we call the *Resurrection*. They are *witnesses* to all of this.

They are also witnesses to something else, a teaching that really angered and upset people—the idea that to be one of God's people, you don't have to be born into a certain family or nation. You just have to believe in Jesus, and follow him. This was God's plan all along, and now the disciples are going to be witnesses to it. They are going to take God's message—of Jesus' resurrection—to *all* people, first in Jerusalem, then in the surrounding area, and, finally, to the whole world. They are continuing the story Jesus began. Like Jesus, the disciples will have enemies—people who do not want their message to spread, people who will even try to kill them for it.

But they are not alone as they continue Jesus' story. Jesus promises them that his Holy Spirit, the Holy Spirit of God, will be with them. And Jesus' resurrection promises that even their suffering—even their *death*—will be redeemed, undone, and made new.

Lesson 2

Acts 1:9-14

Gone But *Not* Gone

What the Parent Should Know: When we read certain passages of the Bible—for example, texts dealing with the Crucifixion, or this text, which deals with what has been called the Ascension—it is essential to remember that the disciples did not have access to what we already know. At the Crucifixion, they had no thought of the Resurrection; even though Jesus had hinted at it strongly, they didn't quite understand. Likewise, in Acts 1, the disciples didn't seem to know that Jesus' presence among them was on the verge of a drastic change.

As anyone familiar with the Old Testament and the Gospels knows, the belief that God would eventually restore his people, that is, "restore the kingdom to Israel," was central and long-held. The faithful believers expected

God to oust the Gentile overlords and establish a lasting, peaceful, and prosperous kingdom centered in Jerusalem. The disciples are there in Jerusalem, waiting and wanting to know: Is this going to happen now? Jesus tells them that it's not for them to know the "times or dates," but that they have work to do, and they will receive power when the Holy Spirit comes upon them.

And then he disappears from their sight, enveloped in a cloud.

It is important, first, to point out that the disciples emphatically did not imagine that Jesus was a space traveler, moving up through the sky, into the atmosphere and stratosphere, and out into space. When contemporary people think of "heaven," we often think of a place that's somewhere up in the sky, where people are floating on clouds, and possibly flying. But despite this persistent misconception, in the Bible "heaven" means God's kingdom, the "place" where God's reign is perfect and all is as it should be. Jesus teaches his disciples to pray for God's will to be done "on earth as it is in heaven." Following Jesus means somehow participating in the life of God's kingdom—the kingdom of heaven—while still occupying this space, where we only see glimpses of what God's kingdom is like.

So why would Jesus leave his disciples and go to that place without them?

In fact, the Ascension does not mean that Jesus is gone. The scholar N.T. Wright points out that the disciples—and early readers of Luke-Acts who were familiar with the Old Testament—would have, on witnessing the Ascension, thought immediately of the vision in Daniel 7. This vision is of a person "like a son of man" who comes "with the clouds of heaven" unto "the Ancient of Days," and is given "authority, glory, and sovereign power; all nations and peoples of every language worshiped him. His dominion is an everlasting dominion that will not pass away, and his kingdom is one that will never be destroyed." (Daniel 7:13-14) Jesus is not leaving; he is being crowned the eternal king of the universe, and his disciples will now become apostles—messengers sent out to the uttermost parts of the kingdom—all the earth, in this case—to proclaim his kingship.

Jesus is leaving, and yet not really leaving. Scholar Luke Timothy Johnson points out that in 2 Kings 2, when the prophet Elijah ascends to heaven "in a whirlwind," his disciple, Elisha, asks for and is granted a "double portion" of Elijah's prophetic spirit, and then takes up Elijah's mantle (robe) and continues his prophetic ministry. (We still sometimes use the phrase "take up the mantle" to indicate the continuance of a particular kind of work in the tradition of the one who began, or last carried out, that work.)

The coming of the Holy Spirit is akin to this, and so we are to understand that the disciples are in fact carrying on Jesus' ministry filled with his Spirit. His promise in what Christians have come to call "the great commission"

(Matthew 28:20) to be *"with you always, to the very end of the age"* is not voided by the Ascension. He is not gone, but present in a new way.

The disciples—now apostles—meanwhile, carry on his ministry filled with his Spirit and in prayerful obedience, with the hope that *"this same Jesus, who has been taken from you into heaven, will come back in the same way you have seen him go into heaven,"* as they saw him go (Acts 1:11). And when he does, heaven—where God is—and earth—where we are—we be united as one forever. For now, Christians pray *"Your kingdom come, your will be done . . ."* proclaiming Christ's kingship and doing the work of the kingdom.

Begin by reading aloud:

Even if you are a child, you know that this world you live in has problems in it. Things go wrong. People get hurt and sick; people feel sad; people hurt one another; people are greedy and selfish. Things aren't all as they should be—things are neither as we would like them to be nor as God would like them to be.

But Jesus' disciples, along with God's people throughout many long years, were waiting for God to establish his kingdom. They were waiting for someone—whom they often called the *Messiah*—who would be their king, rescuing them from the sometimes-brutal foreign rule they'd been living under for hundreds of years. The kingdom that God would establish for them would have its center in the city of Jerusalem, and it would be a place of peace and prosperity where there is no more hurting, no more sickness, no more sadness, and no more greed, nor selfishness, nor people hurting other people. When Jesus came, and people began to realize that he was the Messiah, they were constantly surprised by what he meant by the "kingdom." He was not going to start a war and take over the land that had been promised to God's people. Instead, God's kingdom was going to be something else altogether.

And of course, people's hopes that Jesus would establish this kingdom were crushed when Jesus died. But here, in this story, Jesus is alive again, and he has been with the disciples for forty days, showing that he was really and truly alive again, and teaching them more about God's kingdom.

But they are still waiting—in Jerusalem, no less, the very place where they expected God's good kingdom to begin—and they want to know: *Is this really going to happen? Is it going to happen* now?

Jesus' answer is surprising and probably not very satisfying to them. He tells them they can't know the answer to that question, but they will get power from the Holy Spirit of God, and they will "be his witnesses" throughout all the earth.

And then he disappears from their sight, enveloped in a cloud!

What is happening here? Has Jesus turned into some kind of space traveler, traveling up through the layers of the atmosphere and into outer space? No, he has not. While we sometimes think of "heaven" as a place "up there in the sky," the writers of the Bible did not think of it that way. In the Bible, heaven means God's kingdom, the place where everything is as it should be. You may have heard the Lord's Prayer, which asks God to make things on earth as they are in heaven. And that is what the disciples were waiting for: God's peaceful and prosperous kingdom to be on earth. But then, instead of saying, "Yes, that kingdom is starting now," Jesus leaves—in a cloud—and goes to where God is! He seems to be gone!

But Jesus is not *really* gone. Before this, he had promised his disciples that he would be with them always, and he is not breaking his promise.

In a book of the Old Testament (the only part of the Bible that Jesus' disciples had and knew) called Daniel, there is the story of a person who comes to heaven in a cloud and is made king of all the earth, of "all peoples, nations, and languages" for always and always. The disciples now see that Jesus is not leaving them, not really. He is being crowned king of the universe, and they are being sent as his messengers to take the news that Jesus is King to everyone in the world.

Another story in the Old Testament—this time, one that comes from 2 Kings 2—helps us to understand the meaning of Jesus' *ascension*— which is the word that Christians have used to talk about the moment at which Jesus went up to heaven in the cloud. In 2 Kings, a prophet—a special messenger of God who had been given the ability to speak to God's people with God's strength and power—named Elijah is taken up to heaven in much the same way that Jesus is taken up to heaven. Elijah has a disciple, too, called Elisha. As Elijah is leaving, Elisha asks that he be given some of Elijah's power as a prophet of God. Elisha gets this, and then he picks up Elijah's mantle (a sort of coat or robe) and goes on with the work Elijah had already been doing. Even today, you may sometimes hear people speak of "taking up the mantle" of someone else. It means that the person will continue the work started by another person.

And in fact this is what the disciples have to do. They must take up Jesus' mantle and continue Jesus' work—announcing that Jesus *is* King and that, one day, when Jesus returns in the same way that he left, God's kingdom (heaven) and this earth (where we are now, where there are problems of all kinds) will be made into one kingdom, forever and ever.

Meanwhile, the disciples, who we will soon learn to call "apostles" (more on that in the next lesson) are, like Elisha carrying on Elijah's

Lesson 2: Gone but *not* Gone

ministry, continuing Jesus' work. The Holy Spirit comes upon them, and they travel and pray and work as they wait for the day when Jesus will return to be king of a new heaven and earth, which will no longer be separate, where all things will be as they ought to be, with no one going hungry, no one hurting anyone else, and people living peacefully with one another.

And that is why Christians, even today, pray for God's will to be done, and for God's kingdom to come. That is why Christians try to do what is kind and right and what pleases God: because we are trying to take up Jesus' mantle.

And we are not doing it all on our own: Jesus is gone, but he is not *really* gone. His Spirit is with us still, as it always will be. And one day, he will be back; God's space and ours will be one space, and all will be as it should be.

Lesson 3

Acts 1

What is an Apostle?

What the Parent Should Know: In Greek, "apostle" simply means "one who is sent on a mission."

It is sometimes easy to forget that what we now consider rudimentary communication devices—the telegraph, for example—are astonishingly new: in the ancient world, news was limited to what a person, or group of people, could pass on either by word of mouth or by carrying messages written on papyrus or pieces of broken pottery. These messengers carried important news, such as news of wars won or lost, or news of a new king. And these messengers might have been called apostles.

In the New Testament, "apostle" is sometimes used to refer only to the twelve disciples (minus Judas, plus Matthias—more on that in a moment) who testified to Jesus' resurrection. But other times—especially in Paul's letters (or "epistles"), apostle means any person who has seen the risen Christ. Paul himself qualifies as an apostle because he saw a vision of the risen Christ. But perhaps the most important point to make about an apostle is the apostle's message. What are the New Testament apostles sent to proclaim? They are sent to proclaim the news that the risen Christ is King.

Scholars such as N.T. Wright have observed that the number of the disciples (twelve) matches that of the tribes of Israel. After the defection of Judas Iscariot, whom, we are told in this chapter, dies rather gruesomely as a "reward for his wickedness," the number had to be brought back up to twelve in order to preserve that symbolic integrity. This was accomplished by choosing from among the group of people who had accompanied Jesus and his disciples from the time of John's baptism, and, importantly, who had been witnesses to the Resurrection. Two were nominated: Joseph (called Barsabbas or Justus) and Matthias. With prayer, the disciples asked God to make his will clear through the drawing of lots. This may seem to contemporary readers a rather unspiritual way of deciding a matter (akin to rolling dice), but in the ancient world, drawing lots was considered a way for God to make his will known. (See, for example, Proverbs 16:33, which reads, "The lot is cast into the lap, but its every decision is from the LORD.")

There is no good reason to think that the twelve apostles are meant to replace the twelve tribes of Israel—it's probably better to think that they're renewing it. The renewing of Israel has preoccupied the devout all throughout the Gospels, and this preoccupation continues here, when the disciples ask whether Jesus is now going to restore the kingdom to Israel. But Jesus' answer is confusing, as anyone familiar with the Gospels might expect. It's not for them to know the "when" of it all, Jesus says, but rather, they are to be his witnesses in the world through the power given to them by the Holy Spirit. This is why they are called apostles—like other ancient apostles, they were officially charged with spreading the news of the newly crowned king: the king of all the earth, who has conquered even death itself.

But this is not the kind of king—or kingdom—the apostles were expecting. It is rather a disappointment to them to realize that Jesus does not intend to overthrow Caesar's government and set up his own. Jesus is King, but all is not as God wishes it to be on earth (as it is in heaven). The disciples/apostles, like us, are still waiting for God's kingdom to come completely; for God to bind up all wounds and wipe every tear. Yet by proclaiming Jesus' resurrection, the apostles are making it known that Jesus is King: that God's kingdom has broken into the kingdom of this world, vanquishing that power no earthly king or emperor, however mighty, could control: death.

We should note, finally, that the apostles are a ragtag group. They are ordinary people, and their message is accepted earliest and most eagerly by the people then considered lowliest: women, slaves, and the very poor. Yet the apostles have something remarkable: the presence of God's Holy Spirit as well as God's power. And, perhaps most remarkably, they are eyewitnesses to the resurrected Jesus, whom they have seen and touched; with whom they have broken bread. *While Christians today often fixate on Jesus' death as the center of the story, the apostles regarded the Resurrection as the center. It declared definitively that Jesus was King of the only Kingdom with any real power.*

This is the truth that the sent-out ones, the apostles, are bringing to the world: Jesus has risen from the dead. Jesus is King.

Begin by reading aloud:

Have you ever talked on the telephone to someone who lived very far away? Maybe you have used a computer or another kind of device that allowed you actually to see and hear the person to whom you were talking. Some children live very far away from their grandparents or other relatives, and they are thankful for these kinds of things, which allow them to share all their news.

These same machines—telephones, computers, and other devices— also make it possible for news to travel very quickly from one part of the world to the other. When a war begins (or ends) on one side of the world, we can know about it almost instantly, even if we are thousands and thousands of miles away. But in the ancient world, the world in which Jesus lived, none of these things existed.

Instead, in the ancient world, news was mostly limited to what a person, or group of people, could pass on by what we call "word of mouth;" that is, one person telling another person and that person telling another person, and so on. (Sometimes people also carried messages written on papyrus or pieces of broken pottery, but even so, the pottery had to be carried by messengers.) In the language spoken by the people who wrote the New Testament—the part of the Bible where we find the book of Acts—these messengers were known as *apostles.*

Imagine for a moment that a teacher came to your town to teach you and a group of your friends how to play a new kind of game or how to make a new kind of craft. And then, after the teacher left, she instructed you to travel around your own town and even beyond your town, teaching other children everything that she had taught you. You would then be a sort of apostle: a person sent out to share a kind of message or lesson with other people. If you can imagine that, you can easily understand what Luke and the other New Testament writers mean when they say *apostle.*

In the New Testament, the word apostle can mean any of the people who saw Jesus after his resurrection. It can also mean the special group of twelve people that were with Jesus for all of his time on earth, until the time he was taken up into heaven. Going back to the imaginary teacher who came to your town to teach you a game or craft, you might imagine that she had twelve *official* students—students whom she had specially chosen—but that many more students actually tagged along to learn from her. If you can imagine that, you will understand what it was like when Jesus was traveling and teaching. He had twelve *special* students, but many other people followed along to learn from him.

Perhaps you remember the story about Judas, who was the one of Jesus' disciples who chose to betray him—that is, to help Jesus' enemies capture Jesus. The beginning of Acts tells us what happens to Judas, and I'm afraid it isn't very pleasant at all. With the money he got from betraying Jesus, Judas bought a field, and in the field he died in a messy and bloody way. This meant that there were, in fact, only eleven disciples left. But that's not good—there needed to be twelve special apostles to carry the message about Jesus. But why? Why *twelve*?

Luke, the writer of Acts, is trying to show us something important with this number twelve. In the long-ago days of God's people Israel, there were twelve tribes. Through a number of terrible events, the twelve tribes were scattered, and God's people were waiting for God to restore—rebuild, remake, regather—the kingdom of Israel. By making sure that there are *twelve* apostles, Luke is trying to point out that God is using these people to rebuild God's kingdom, although not in the way they expect. So, praying and asking God to show them whom they should choose as the twelfth apostle, they choose a man called Matthias, who was among the group of people (in addition to the original twelve) who'd followed Jesus around, learning from him, and who had seen him after his resurrection.

So when Bible writers use the word apostle, they mean a person who was sent out to share the message—the news that they had seen happen right before their eyes—that Jesus had risen from the dead. And in saying that, they were saying something very important—that *Jesus is King.* That is why there must be twelve apostles: to show that God's people and God's kingdom *is* being rebuilt, but in a new way. By rising from the dead, Jesus has shown that God's kingdom is more powerful than any earthly king or emperor. No earthly king or emperor can overcome the power of death—but Jesus did.

The apostles were ordinary people, but Luke tells us that they have God's Holy Spirit upon them as well as God's power within them. And they have seen something remarkable: Jesus crucified, dead, buried, and then *alive again.* He had been dead, but he had returned, and they had touched him, talked with him, eaten with him. Now, before returning to heaven—the place where everything is already as God wants things to be everywhere, with no death, no pain, and no sadness—Jesus sends his friends out to be *apostles*: messengers with an astonishing message: Jesus has risen from the dead, and Jesus is King—Jesus is *the* King.

Lesson 4

Acts 2:22-41
God's Deliverance: The Exodus, Jesus, and Evil

What the Parent Should Know: This section of Peter's sermon in Acts 2 is as theologically dense as it is rhetorically powerful. Not only does it offer a robust exposition on the meaning of Jesus' death in relation to both divine and human intentions, but it also defends Christ's kingship from the Old Testament and offers an invitation to his hearers—mainly "Israelites" to "repent and be baptized"—while emphasizing that this invitation is not only for them, but for whomever God may call.

Peter argues that Jesus' "miracles, wonders, and signs" clearly marked him as sent by God; but that, nonetheless, even the very people who witnessed those affirmations handed him over to be crucified. It is important to acknowledge here that some Christians throughout history have used this (and similar New Testament pronouncements) as justification for anti-Semitism. But that is a gross misrepresentation of what Peter actually says in this text (and let us not forget that Peter himself denied Jesus three times and thus had a measure of complicity in his death as well). Peter does not mince words, but he does address the situation with far greater nuance than later anti-Semitic slurs accusing Jewish people of being "Christ-killers." Israelites were certainly the ones to reject Jesus, one of their own, and hand him over to the Roman authorities for crucifixion—but Gentiles also cooperated and were just as culpable.

But here is perhaps the most perplexing part: all of this was somehow part of "God's deliberate plan and foreknowledge," a fact that does not mitigate the culpability of the human beings. This endlessly mysterious theological dynamic—which is summed up nicely in Genesis 50:20 ("You intended to harm me, but God intended it for good to accomplish what is now being done, the saving of many lives")—appears throughout the Bible. It appears, for example, in Isaiah 10:5, which paradoxically and confusingly pronounces "Woe to the Assyrian"—referring to the group that is about to attack Israel—while simultaneously calling the Assyrians "the rod of my anger, in whose hand is the club of my wrath!" In other words, the Bible, at various points, and certainly in Peter's sermon here, claims that even those things that human beings intend for evil are used—intended, even—by God for good.

None of this is easy for contemporary readers to wrap their minds around, of course, and it is ultimately an insoluble mystery. What is unambiguous, however, is that Jesus has been raised from the dead and has conquered the forces of death, and is now exalted as the King of the universe. Considering his audience (again, mostly Israelites), it is no surprise that Peter argues vigorously for Jesus' kingship from the Old Testament—the only Bible his hearers had and knew. The heart of this section quotes Psalm 16, which itself emphasizes that God "will not abandon [his anointed] to the realm of the dead, nor will [he] let [his] faithful one see decay." The psalm is traditionally attributed to and understood to refer to David, but Peter points out that it can't really be talking about David, because David has long been dead.

Still, Israelites would have been familiar with the promise of 2 Samuel 7: that a son of David would one day occupy the throne at God's right hand. Peter is therefore arguing that David's words should be read as prophetic. He is arguing in terms his audience would hear as proof beyond a reasonable doubt that Jesus is the rightful heir of David and that even the cooperative wickedness of Jews and Gentiles was no match for God's power. Peter is obviously trying to elicit a response from his audience, for he concludes his argument by asserting that "God has made this Jesus, whom you crucified, both Lord and Messiah."

These words cut his hearers to the heart and prompt them to ask what they should do. "Repent and be baptized, every one of you, in the name of Jesus Christ for the forgiveness of your sins." Repent simply means "turn back and go in the opposite direction." Baptism has at least a double significance. It is a reminder of Israel's passage through the Red Sea in Exodus, when God mightily delivered his people from slavery; now he is delivering them from slavery to sin and from the inevitable death that awaits us all, by the promise of Jesus' resurrection. Baptism is also a picture of Christ's death, burial, and resurrection. It is a rite, a way of marking oneself as being in Christ and part of the new community of his followers.

Significantly, though he has opened by addressing Israelites, Peter closes by affirming that the promise of forgiveness of sins and the gift of the Holy Spirit is not only for them but is "for all whom the Lord our God will call."

Peter has persuasively shown that God's long plan of deliverance, intimated throughout the Bible, has come to its most crucial point and it is a good and hopeful promise not only for Israel, but for whomever will listen and respond.

Begin by reading aloud:

If you have ever been to a church service, you probably noticed that there's a time during each service for a *sermon*, a talk based on some part of the Bible. The book of Acts contains a lot of sermons because, as you'll remember, the disciples—now called apostles—have been given the job of continuing Jesus' own work now that Jesus has ascended to heaven, which, you'll also remember, doesn't mean "a place up in the sky" but rather "where God is." In these sermons, the apostles try to persuade people that Jesus is the true king, and that, because he's the true king, *his* authority matters more than any other rules made by any other ruler.

The sermon Peter preaches in this chapter is similar to others throughout the book of Acts. In this case, he's speaking to a large group of Israelites—and explaining from their Bible (the Old Testament) that Jesus, is, in fact, the one they have been waiting and hoping for during many, many, *many* long years.

Some of what Peter says in this section is very hard for the people to hear. For example, he points out that the "miracles, wonders, and signs" of Jesus made it very obvious that he was the one sent to them by God. But not only did they not believe that Jesus was sent by God, they handed him over to the Roman authorities to be crucified. Yet, Peter says, all of that was somehow part of "God's deliberate plan." God knew all along that Jesus would be killed, and that he would raise him from the dead.

This is a very strange teaching and one that no one has ever quite solved. But it is all throughout the Bible. You may, for example, have heard the story of Joseph. His brothers, jealous that their father loved Joseph more than he loved the rest of them, sold Joseph into slavery. Through a series of events, Joseph becomes a powerful man in Egypt, and, years after they treated him so horribly, Joseph's brothers travel to Egypt in search of food; there is a famine in their own land, but, thanks to Joseph's wisdom and planning, there is a huge quantity of grain stored in Egypt. Joseph's brothers don't recognize Joseph, but accept food from him. Later, when they realize who has saved their lives by giving them food, and after their father has died, Joseph's brothers beg for forgiveness. They're afraid that Joseph will kill them in revenge. But Joseph tells them not to be afraid, because even though they intended to harm him, God meant it for good all along. Because they sold him into slavery—and because of all the other things that happened along the way—he was able to save their lives when they would have died from starvation. "Don't be afraid," he tells them. "I will provide for you and your children."

We should not think that the people who killed Jesus—and handed Jesus over to be killed—were somehow doing a *good* thing. Joseph's brothers did not do a good thing, even if it worked out well in the end that Joseph ended up in Egypt. When a person does evil to another person and it works out somehow to a good result—let's say you push your little brother over in the yard and when he falls, he suddenly finds your mother's lost wedding ring—the result is good (the wedding ring is found!) but pushing your little brother over was still wrong. The people who killed Jesus were not doing a good thing, and no one—not Peter, not God—is saying that they were. But here is the tricky thing: in the Joseph story, in Peter's sermon, and in other places in the Bible, we are told that God uses even those things that human beings intend for evil—things that *are* evil—for good.

Do you find that difficult to understand? If you do, that's normal. Many, many, *many* people have tried to figure out this particular Bible teaching and can't seem to do it.

But that is not the only thing Peter's sermon is about. Peter also points out that the Bible the Israelites had—the Hebrew Bible or what Christians usually call the Old Testament—promises that one day, an heir of King David would come and reign forever. One of the psalms that David wrote promised that God's "anointed one" would not "see decay" or stay "in the realm of the dead." People thought of *David* as the Anointed One, but as Peter points out, David has been dead and buried for many, many years. David wasn't talking about himself. He was talking about Jesus, who came hundreds of years after David had died. Peter closes his sermon by saying that "God has made this Jesus, whom you crucified, both Lord and Messiah."

How do you think the people listening to Peter's sermon felt, hearing all of this? They had been waiting for so long for the promised one—the heir of David—to come, and when he had come, they hadn't really recognized him. More than that, they'd cheered when the Romans put him to death. *They'd* crucified him!

"What should we *do?*" the people cried.

Peter tells them: "Repent and be baptized, every one of you, in the name of Jesus Christ for the forgiveness of your sins." *Repent* simply means: "turn back and go the other way." Realize that you have been rejecting and running from Jesus, and run to him and accept him instead.

Perhaps you already know what it means to *be baptized*. In some churches being baptized means being sprinkled with a bit of water; in others, it means being dipped completely under the water. Either way, the water of baptism reminds us of several important things. First, it reminds us of God delivering his people from slavery in Egypt by parting the Red Sea. Second, it reminds us of Jesus' death, burial, and resurrection. Finally, baptism also is a way of showing that we are a part of the new family God is making through Jesus.

It is important to notice that although he began his sermon talking mostly to Israelites—Jewish people—Peter closes his sermon by saying that the promise of being forgiven from sins and the promise of the Holy Spirit are *not* only for Israelites, but are for *anyone and everyone*—"all whom the Lord our God will call." God is able to take even the most evil things—the death of Jesus, the terrible things people do to one another—and work them out for good.

Even more than that, God is able to *forgive* people for the terrible things they do, and promise them a new kind of life in Jesus.

Unit 2

The Holy Spirit

The Holy Spirit is the third person of the triune God, and the Holy Spirit is imagined in the New Testament as something like a wind, or a fire. The Holy Spirit, Jesus says, is who will be with his followers to help them spread the news that Jesus has conquered death and that he is the Lord. And the Holy Spirit, Jesus promises in the Gospels, is the presence of God dwelling in each of us—temples of the Holy Spirit—as unlikely and surprising as that may seem. As New Testament scholar N.T. Wright has put it, all of this is somewhat mysterious, but it is an indication of the strange but wonderful reality that those who have the Holy Spirit within them are themselves the temple of God. They—WE, if we are Christians—are places where heaven and earth meet.

I have heard it said that the book of Acts would more accurately be called "The Acts of the Apostles Through the Help of the Holy Spirit." Indeed, it is because of the Holy Spirit that the apostles are able to heal disease and infirmity. It is because of the Holy Spirit that they are able to endure suffering with joy. The Holy Spirit may be quiet as wind, but the Holy Spirit is astonishing in power. And the Holy Spirit dwells in each person who believes in Jesus.

What the Parent Should Know: Pentecost is fifty days after Passover and has, in Judaism, a double significance. First, it is the feast of first fruits: farmers would bring in the first sheaf of wheat from their harvest and offer it to God in thanksgiving and also in the hope that the rest of the harvest would be safely gathered in. Pentecost is also traditionally understood as the day that Moses received the law on Mount Sinai. Both of these are significant to understanding the meaning of "Pentecost" as Christians usually mean it—the day shortly after Jesus' ascension when the Holy Spirit descended upon the apostles in "tongues of fire," causing them to speak in languages they hadn't previously known or learned.

That the Holy Spirit descends in this way at this time is important for a pragmatic reason: lots of people—"God-fearing Jews from every nation under heaven"—were staying in Jerusalem for the celebration of the feast of Pentecost. Jesus had charged the apostles with preaching the Gospel to everyone, everywhere, and what better way to spread the word quickly than with an astonishing display of the Holy Spirit's power before a great gathering?

The coming of the Holy Spirit at the time of Pentecost is also meaningful because it invites us to recognize what is happening as the first fruits of God's new work in the risen and exalted Christ and through the Holy Spirit: there will be more to come.

Further, that Pentecost is the day Moses received the law from God is notable because a similar thing is happening here in Acts. God descends on Mount Sinai "in fire" (Exodus 18), and the Holy Spirit descends upon the apostles in tongues of fire; Moses brings the Word of God to the people, as do the apostles. Jesus has ascended as Moses did and sent his Holy Spirit "down" with word and power. That the Spirit comes from heaven "like the blowing of a violent wind" is significant: numerous places in Scripture describe God's power as a "wind."

But Pentecost may also remind readers of what happened at Babel (Genesis 11) when God confused the common language of people attempting to ascend to heaven on their own terms: a kind of blasphemy. Here, the Holy Spirit of God descends upon people and makes possible a miraculous kind of understanding: Babel in reverse.

Not surprisingly, the people who witnessed the apostles' speaking in tongues found the display amazing as well as perplexing, and were sure that it had some significance. Others, however, made fun of them and assumed that they were drunk. Peter explains that what is happening is a fulfillment of something that God has promised in Scripture: here, now, have come the "last days" in which God's Spirit is poured out on "all people," and "everyone who calls on the name of the Lord will be saved."

This is both a fulfillment of God's promise to Abraham in Genesis 12—which, not incidentally, happens right after the Babel fiasco—that "all nations" of the earth would be blessed through him, and of Jesus' many declarations that the Gospel is for all people.

Pentecost, is, then, the first fruits of that mission to all people. God's salvation and the gift of the Holy Spirit is not for a few. It is for everyone *who calls on the name of the Lord.*

Begin by reading aloud:

If you were to go to New York City, to the headquarters of the United Nations (U.N.), and into a room where one of the U.N. sessions was being held, you would see people in booths, wearing headphones and speaking into microphones. When someone says something in a meeting of the U.N., they speak into a special sort of microphone. If they are speaking English, everyone in the room who understands English will hear their words directly in their headphones. But when someone speaks a different language, the people in booths interpret it as quickly as possible for those who do not understand that language, while other interpreters translate those words into still *other* languages, which goes into the headphones of the people who understand those languages. It is quite a complicated system, depending on both machines and people working well, but it is necessary in order for the U.N. to function, since there are people from so many different countries—who speak so many different languages—at the U.N.

Right after Jesus ascended into heaven, the Holy Spirit of God descended—that is, came down on—the apostles, just as Jesus had promised would happen. A great wind came—which in the Bible is often a sign that God's presence is coming in a special way—and bits of fiery flame shaped like tongues appeared over their heads. We call this day *Pentecost*. Some churches celebrate Pentecost every year. In a church I once attended, the children made little crowns with red paper flames shaped like tongues attached, which they wore in order to look how the apostles might have looked when the Holy Spirit came upon them. Why were the bits of flame shaped like tongues? Perhaps to show the amazing power that the Holy Spirit gave to them: they were all able to speak in languages that they hadn't previously known or learned.

But before Pentecost meant "the day that the Holy Spirit came down," it was *another* kind of religious festival. The name "Pentecost" means "fiftieth day," because Pentecost was the fiftieth day after Passover, and *that* was the festival of Shavuot [sha-vooh-oht]. On that day, Jewish farmers would bring in the first sheaf, or bundle, from their wheat harvest, and offer it to God as a way of thanking God for bringing forth the harvest, and as a way of expressing their hope that the rest of the crop would be brought in safely. This day was also believed to be the day that Moses had received the law from God when he went up on a mountain called Sinai.

Because it was a festival day, there were gathered in Jerusalem many people from many different regions where many different languages were spoken. You will remember from an earlier lesson that Jesus had told his disciples to be his witnesses in Jerusalem, Judea, Samaria, and to the farthest parts of the earth. But before they even left Jerusalem, people from all those places came to *them*, and the apostles were able to tell them about Jesus in all their different languages, even though they'd never spoken those languages before! Most of the people were amazed and couldn't imagine what this strange episode might mean. Some of the people even thought that the apostles had been drinking too much wine, and were just babbling nonsense.

But that's not at all what was happening. Peter jumps up to explain how what is happening is actually God making good on a promise he had made a long time ago: here and now have come the "last days" in which God's Spirit is poured out on "all people" so that "everyone who calls on the name of the Lord will be saved." In other words, everyone who recognizes Jesus as the Lord of all will participate in the new kind of life and new kind of world that Jesus and his followers are building.

Before, Moses had gone up onto the mountain to receive God's words from God. Now, God's Spirit is coming down to fill people with God's words.

Before, some people assumed that God's presence was just for *them:* because of the family they had been born into, because of how wealthy and important they were, or because of how rigorously they followed all the rules.

And the remarkable miracle of speaking in tongues is only the beginning—the first fruits of the harvest. The apostles, speaking the languages of *all* the people, are showing and telling that God's salvation and the gift of the Holy Spirit is not for a select group of people: it is for everyone who believes that Jesus is Lord of all.

Lesson 6

Acts 3
Making All Things New: Times of Refreshing

What the Parent Should Know: This story is the subject of a popular children's Sunday School song: "Peter and John went to pray/They met a lame man on the way/He put out his palm, and asked them for alms/And this is what Peter did say . . ." The children often enjoy finishing the song by enacting its chorus: "He went jumping and leaping and praising God." Based on the preceding passage, we can assume that the healing of the man lame from birth was one of the "many signs and wonders being done by the apostles."

Because almsgiving was (and is) an important religious duty within Judaism, it's no surprise that this man spent his days by the temple gate. This was an accepted and common way for a disabled person to support himself—one that continues in many parts of the world to this day. In the absence of formal programs to assist disabled people, laying them in a place where they could beg for alms was often the best the culture could do; some scholars suggest that destitute and disabled people often fared better among settlements of Jews than in other places because of the imperative for almsgiving.

Although contemporary Westerners frequently look askance at begging—often assuming that the one begging could and should simply take measures to improve his own lot in life, rather than asking for money from others—Peter and John would likely have seen nothing unusual in it. And there is no reason to think that the church was at all averse to giving to the needy. On the contrary, as the previous verses (Acts 2:44-5) indicate, money and possessions were held lightly and shared freely among the community of believers (and presumably to those outside, as other texts in Acts, such as 6:1, suggest).

Yet Peter and John have something much better to give to this man. Alms might relieve his suffering for the moment or for the day, but they have something much better to give him: healing and freedom from his congenital and permanent disability; a dignity and wholeness he had never known—"in the name of Jesus Christ of Nazareth, rise up and walk." (To invoke someone's name was to invoke that person's power.) And, with a hand from Peter, the man gets to his feet, jumping and leaping and praising God, to the astonishment of everyone within sight of this remarkable scene.

Never one to let a teaching opportunity slip by, Peter launches into a sermon there in the portico of the temple. It is a remarkably direct, even harsh sermon, in which he asks, basically, why in the world these people are at all amazed at what has happened, as though it were owing to their own power that the man had been healed. Do they not realize that what has happened is all through the power of Jesus' name—the same Jesus that they have just handed over to death at the hands of the Romans, though he himself was and is the author—that is, the initiator and source—of life? But God's power is so great that God raised him from the dead, and it is this same resurrection power that is at work here: faith in Jesus' name has made a man crippled from birth more whole than he had ever been before.

Peter then invites his hearers to repent "so that times of refreshing" may come from God. Jesus must remain "in heaven" (that is, God's space) until the time of a future restoration that will be universal and complete. But the healing of the man and the promise of times of refreshing suggest that God's resurrection power is already at work. Peter concludes by insisting that Jesus is the "prophet like Moses" that the Scriptures foretold; the one that all the prophets spoke of, the one who would ultimately fulfill God's promise to Abraham, that through his descendants "all the families of the earth" would be blessed.

God in Jesus Christ has undone the worst thing that can happen: death itself. There is nothing he cannot conquer. People have only to call on his name.

Begin by reading aloud:

Have you ever seen a person begging for money on the street? It is always sad and sometimes even a little scary to see. Most often, people who beg for money on the street do so because they are unwell in some way: either in their minds or in their bodies. Outside one of the shops near my home some men whose legs don't work sit each day, begging for money. Their upper bodies are strong and normal-sized, but their legs are very small and twisted. Some of them became ill with a virus that stopped their legs from growing properly, but others were born that way.

In many countries today, people with disabilities don't have to sit outside and beg for money, because there are programs in churches and community centers that help people who aren't able to work. But in poor countries today, there are still many people who have few choices other than supporting themselves through begging. And in the disciples' time, that was how people who were disabled survived. Because it was important to Jewish people to help those in need, poor people and disabled people often got along much better in Jewish areas than in other places.

Perhaps that's why the disabled man—Luke, the author, tells us that the man couldn't walk, and had been disabled from the time of his birth—sat every day in front of the temple: the people going in there each day would have seen it as their duty to give something to this unfortunate man. So when Peter and John are on their way to the temple to pray, the disabled man asks them for alms. They don't have any money, but they have something much, much better: through Jesus' name—meaning, through Jesus' power—they tell him to get up and walk, and he *does!* Can you imagine it? He has never walked in his whole life, and then, all of a sudden, at a word, at a touch from Peter, he gets to his feet, walking, leaping, jumping, and praising God. He knows whose power has healed him.

Some money might have relieved the man's hard life for a day or two, but Peter has *healed* him from the problem that had him begging in the first place. This was a remarkable thing, and everyone who saw it was astonished.

Peter, who was great at taking every opportunity to talk to people about Jesus, immediately begins preaching a sermon. "Why are you amazed at *this?*" he says. "It's not as though it's *our* power has healed the man! It's all because of Jesus—the same Jesus whom you handed over to be killed." Jesus was the "author of life," which means the source of all life, and they had him killed. But God raised him from the dead, and it is that same power, that resurrection power, and the disabled man's faith in it, that has healed him.

Peter tells the people he understands they didn't know what they were doing when they handed Jesus over to be killed, and that God's chosen one would come and suffer was a fact that the Old Testament had made very clear. But even if they didn't know what they were doing, Peter says, they need to repent, so that "times of refreshing" may come from God. Jesus is going to remain "in heaven" (not up in the sky, but in God's space) for a given period of time, until he returns to make everything as it should be, but God's amazing power—the same power that raised Jesus from the dead and the disabled man from the ground—is already working and active. Peter says this power is available to those who repent of the wrong things they've done and believe that Jesus is the one sent by God and the author—or source—of life itself.

Lesson 6: Making All Things New: Times of Refreshing

God in Jesus Christ has undone the worst thing that can happen: death itself. There is nothing else that he cannot conquer. People have only to call on his name—to believe that he is the powerful author of life, and to ask for his help.

Lesson 7

Galatians 5-6; and Romans 8

Life in the Spirit

What the Parent Should Know: This lesson draws from two related passages in the Apostle Paul's letters—Galatians 5 and Romans 8—to show what life in the Spirit looks like, particularly as opposed to life under the law, a distinction that Paul is eager to make in both passages.

In the Galatians context, believers had become convinced that they needed to be following the law, particularly as regards circumcision, to be on good terms with God. Paul's intent is to thoroughly refute this idea.

Freedom is a major concern in this passage, as it is in Romans 8: the Spirit sets us free. Because believers' righteousness is in Christ alone, Paul argues, they have only to live into that reality; attempting to keep the law in addition to that is futile and counterproductive—an obstacle, not a pathway, to God.

The law, Paul argues in both places, can lead only to condemnation under that law, since there is no way that it can be kept perfectly anyway. Keeping one part of the law—such as circumcision—means putting one's whole self under all of it. Instead, Paul encourages believers to embrace the freedom for which Christ has set them free: not a freedom to do whatever one pleases, but a freedom to love and to do good to one another without the unbearable constraints and burdens of the law.

"Faith working through love is what counts more than any law-keeping," Paul says. If we are people growing in the Spirit, the fruits of the Spirit will mark our lives: love, joy, peace, patience, and so on. When we are living in this way, Paul says, we aren't subject to the law. But, Paul cautions, beware of envy and competition—perhaps even envy and competition in seeing who is bearing more spiritual fruit than the other.

Such selflessness seems almost unnatural, and it may well be, which is why we need the Spirit's help.

In Romans 8, Paul also affirms that Christ has set believers free from the law, and that they are thus no longer in the flesh, but in the Spirit. The Spirit, Paul says, is the source of eternal life that enables us to bear up in suffering and weakness; that intercedes for us when we have a hard time even knowing what to pray; and who holds us in the durable love of God in Jesus, a love that is, he says, stronger than death itself.

Life in the Holy Spirit looks very different from a life lived according to rules. It is, rather, a life lived in accordance with the radical, self-giving love of Christ. If that seems impossible, it is because it is impossible without the help of Christ's Spirit. This is not a burdensome life of worry. It is, rather, a life in which we're set free to do good to one another without anxiety over God's approval. God has approved us in Christ, and we are set free to do good to one another.

Begin by reading aloud:

Sometimes when older children and younger children play games together, the older children become exasperated with the younger children because the younger children aren't following the rules.

"He's CHEATING!" someone shouts. The younger child gets upset. The older child is angry. And sometimes the adults ask, "Why can't you just let him play the way he wants to, for the sake of peace?"

And *that* suggestion doesn't make the older child very happy. Why should the younger child get a do-over when he makes a mistake, or get to change his move after he's already taken his hand off the game piece? If rules are rules, shouldn't everybody follow all of them all of the time?

In the early days of the church, people often worried about needing to follow the rules that God had put down for his people long ago. Of course, many of Jesus' teachings were all about how following all the right rules isn't the way to God. Jesus himself is the way to God, and he showed us that the meaning and purpose of all of those rules is to love God and love other people, just as the point of rules in a game is to make the game interesting and fun.

Two of the Apostle Paul's letters to early believers remind us of this truth. Perhaps like the parent who encourages the older child to bend the rules for the younger child for the sake of peace (and for the sake of fun, which is, after all, the point of most games), Paul reminds people that they are not under the law any more. Instead of the law—which no one was much good at keeping anyway and which only helped people to judge each other—they have been given the Spirit. And the Spirit, Paul says, gives freedom and life.

Looking at the law, all of us would see all of the ways we don't measure up. But because God in Jesus already accepts us, Paul says, and because we have the Holy Spirit of God in us, we are free from the law and free to do . . . whatever we want?

No! That's not the point at all. Instead, we are free to do good to one another, focusing upon others rather than on ourselves, anxiously, to see whether we've been keeping all the rules or not. It is as if we have already won the game and therefore feel free and generous and willing to let our little brother or sister play it in a way that's not quite following the rules, but isn't, after all, doing any harm, and is also making him or her very happy.

The freedom that comes with the Holy Spirit—Paul calls them the *fruits* of the Spirit—is not a freedom to indulge selfishness. The fruits of the Spirit are in fact the opposite of selfishness—love, joy, peace, patience, goodness, kindness, faithfulness, and self-control.

These things are not easy. It is not always easy to be patient or kind, and sometimes it is very easy to become angry or jealous. That is why we need the special help of the Holy Spirit, who even helps us when we aren't sure how to pray—when we're so frustrated or frightened or tired that we can't even find the words to ask for God's help.

Life in the Spirit means a life in which we are free from the rules that might make it hard for us to love one another. Life in the Spirit means we don't have to worry about earning God's approval, because Jesus has already done that for us. Life in the Spirit means that God, through Jesus, has set us free to do good to one another.

Unit 3

The Cost of Following Jesus

Blessed are you when people insult you, persecute you, and falsely say all kinds of evil against you because of me," Jesus says in Matthew 5:11. "Whoever wants to be my disciple must deny themselves and take up their cross and follow me," he says later in that same Gospel (16:24). The New Testament vision of Christian discipleship involves no shortage of suffering; on the contrary, to follow Jesus is to suffer. "To this you were called," 1 Peter 2:21 reads, "because Christ suffered for you, leaving you an example, that you should follow his steps."

In keeping with its unexpected, seemingly upside-down values, the New Testament consistently envisions suffering as a kind of blessedness. Consider 1 Peter 4:14: "If you are insulted because of the name of Christ, you are blessed, for the Spirit of glory and of God rests on you." Certainly the apostles seem to have understood this paradox, for Acts repeatedly recounts stories of their singing hymns and praying while imprisoned, even going so far as to rejoice over being counted worthy of suffering for the sake of Jesus.

What the Parent Should Know: Following the miraculous healing of the crippled man outside the temple, Peter gives an enthusiastic sermon, at the tail end of which enter "the priests and the captain of the temple guard and the Sadducees." They're anything but pleased to see the apostles teaching, especially because they were "proclaiming in Jesus the resurrection of the dead," and the Sadducees denied the possibility of resurrection from the dead, but also because they did not want anyone who was not part of the educated religious elite to teach. So they put Peter and John in prison for the night. Luke seems eager to emphasize that their arrest did nothing to curb the spread of their message; on the contrary, even as Peter and John are headed to jail, Luke tells us "many who heard the message believed; so the number of men who believed grew to about five thousand."

Peter and John must appear the next day before the "rulers, the elders, and the teachers of the law," along with the high priest, Annas, and members of his family. "By what power or what name did you do this?" they demand to know—Peter and John's subversion of their own religious authority seems to be their preoccupation. Luke is careful to point out—as he often is—that when Peter speaks, he is "filled with the Holy Spirit." Peter's answer is bold, pointed, and full of pathos—"If we are being called to account today for an act of kindness shown to a man who was lame and are being asked how he was healed . . ."—who would be so callous as to take issue with men who have relieved the suffering of a man who'd been lame from birth? But the most important point is that this merciful act was performed "by the name of Jesus Christ of Nazareth, whom [the leaders] crucified but whom God raised from the dead." Peter does not mince words: this miracle was performed in the name of Jesus, whom you killed, and who has risen from the dead, and "salvation is found in no one else." Jesus' name is the only one by which anyone can be saved.

These are hard words for the leaders to hear, especially from Peter and John who are "unschooled, ordinary men." Once again, we can see echoes of Jesus' unexpected way—Jesus chooses unlikely people to perform astonishing signs and to proclaim his message, and it's precisely this reversal of expectations that irritates the authorities, who aren't quite sure what to do with them. "Everyone living in Jerusalem knows they have performed a notable sign, and we cannot deny it," they say. Denial is out, so they will try containment, and command Peter and John not to speak any longer in Jesus' name.

But Peter and John are untroubled by this gag order—"Which is right in God's eyes," they ask, "to listen to you, or to him?" They are unequivocally certain that they have seen and heard the acts and works of God, and that it is the third person of the Trinity, the Holy Spirit, who is strengthening them to speak so boldly even in the face of persecution. All the religious authorities can do, however, is offer empty threats, for to punish them would have been politically inexpedient, as "all the people were praising God for what had happened" [i.e., the healing of the lame man]. So they release Peter and John, who return to "their own people."

Upon their return, Peter and John and their gathered community pray, affirming God's sovereignty and God's identity as the maker of the earth and everything in it. They also invoke Psalm 2—"Why do the nations rage, and the peoples plot in vain?"—interpreting the opposition by the religious authorities that culminated in Jesus' death as an example of "the rulers band[ing] together against the Lord and against his Anointed One." Their prayer seems to move seamlessly from Jesus' persecution and death to their own coming persecution: "Now, Lord, consider their threats and enable your servants to speak your word with great boldness." Their persecution has begun, but they are determined to continue preaching boldly nonetheless.

And God answered their prayer quickly. When they were finished praying, they "were all filled with the Holy Spirit and spoke the Word of God boldly." They were made strong and brave by the ongoing presence of God with them, even in the face of frightening persecution.

Begin by reading aloud:

When Peter and John healed the man who had been crippled from birth—the one who sat every day begging outside the temple gates—they had everyone's attention. Here was this man who had been unable to walk for his entire life, and then, with a few words—"in the name of Jesus Christ of Nazareth, rise up and walk"—the man was on his feet, leaping, and praising God. It is hard to imagine anything more surprising, and so of course everyone was amazed. But, as we saw in a previous lesson, Peter was quick to point out that it wasn't his own power that had healed the man. It was Jesus, who had died and risen again. He had conquered death itself; what more *couldn't* he do?

Not everyone was pleased at what they saw and heard outside the temple: the priests, the temple guard, and the Sadducees (a particular group of religious men who denied the possibility of resurrection from the dead) were not at all happy to see that Peter and John's actions and words were commanding a great deal of attention. They didn't think that anyone outside of their special, educated group should do any teaching at all. Nor were they pleased that Peter was insisting once again that Jesus had risen from the dead, because as I've just mentioned, they thought that the very idea of resurrection was so much nonsense, and just plain wrong. They wanted Peter and John gone, and quickly. So they put them in prison for the night.

But here Luke, the storyteller, is careful to show us that although Peter and John had the misfortune of going to jail, God was already doing good work through them. "Many who heard the message believed," Luke writes, "so the number of men who believed grew to about five thousand." (And that probably doesn't even include the women and children who also came to believe in Jesus at that time.)

The next day, Peter and John have to go before the same religious rulers that put them in jail, in much the same way that a person who is arrested must soon go before a judge who will decide what happens next. These religious leaders seem to be mostly concerned about the fact that Peter and John, as uneducated and poor fisherman, don't have the proper authority to teach the people about religious matters. To the priests, rulers, and teachers, Peter and John are about as worrisome as people who try to act as doctors without having gone to medical school. They are quite certain Peter and John have no business saying anything about God, just as doctors today are quite certain that someone who hasn't studied medicine shouldn't operate on people, or even prescribe pills.

But God loves to work through people whom others—especially those in charge—regard as unworthy. More importantly, Peter and John are confident that they must do the work Jesus gave them to do. And they are sure that the Holy Spirit of God is with them when they are speaking. So although it would have been perfectly natural for Peter to be nervous and frightened as he stood before these important and powerful men, the Holy Spirit enables him to speak bravely. The man was healed "by the name of Jesus Christ of Nazareth," Peter tells them, "whom *you* crucified but whom God raised from the dead. Salvation is found in no one else."

The leaders are shocked at this, because not only do Peter's words contradict what they believe, but Peter himself is an uneducated man. Jesus' unexpected way involved choosing the most unlikely people to perform astonishing signs and proclaim his message, and the authorities find this very, very irritating. *What will we do about these men*, they seem to be asking themselves. Everyone in Jerusalem knows about the miraculous healing of the man who had been crippled from birth, and many people have already come to believe that Jesus has risen from the dead and that he is the rightful king of the world. The leaders know that if they harm Peter and John in some way—or accuse them of lying—many people will protest that they in fact *saw* the man who was born unable to walk, now jumping and leaping. The people will be angry with the rulers if they harm Peter and John, so the most they can do is ask Peter and John to stop speaking about Jesus.

But Peter and John have no intention of doing what the rulers say. "Which is right in God's eyes," they ask, "to listen to you, or to him?" Although these are the same authorities that put Jesus to death, Peter and John are brave. They are not afraid of what these rulers might do to them. They are going to continue speaking about Jesus and listening to God.

When Peter and John return to the rest of their community, they pray together. There have always been people who try to work against what God is doing in the world, they say. Recognizing that they are now part of that work against which people like the religious rulers protest, Peter and John ask God to help them continue speaking God's word boldly. When they finish praying, the house shakes, and the Holy Spirit of God comes to fill each of them, so that they are made strong and brave.

Even though they have begun to suffer for speaking about Jesus, they are determined—and empowered by the Holy Spirit—to continue on.

Lesson 9

Acts 5:17-41

Prison Doors Open

What the Parent Should Know: In a way, this story recapitulates the one in the previous lesson, as it involves a confrontation between the apostles and the religious authorities. The verses that immediately precede this passage (verses 12-16) tell us that the apostles have been busy about their work, preaching the Gospel of the risen Christ and healing many people. They are beginning to garner respect from the people, more and more of whom come to believe in Jesus even as they bring people who are sick and tormented by demons to the apostles for healing and restoration.

Unsurprisingly, this raises the ire and jealousy (v. 17) of the high priest and his party of Sadducees. They arrest and jail the apostles (v.18), but an "angel of the Lord" opens the doors of the jail—perhaps not unlike opening the door to Jesus' tomb—and brings them out, telling them to "go, stand in the temple courts . . . and tell the people all about this new life." So the apostles do just that, entering the temple courts and teaching the people. The boldness of this act can hardly be overstated.

There is a touch of the comedic in the ensuing episode, when "the high priest and his associates" send for the apostles who are not there, but who are in fact "standing in the temple courts teaching the people." The officers "brought the apostles" before the Sanhedrin to be questioned, but Luke carefully notes that "they did not use force, because they feared that the people would stone them." As before, the religious authorities fear the apostles' popular and growing influence.

The high priest's words sound more than a little petulant: "We gave you strict orders not to teach in this name . . . yet you have filled Jerusalem with your teaching and are determined to make us guilty of this man's blood." It is clear that the high priest is understandably exasperated by the apostles' outright defiance, and that he (and, presumably, the other authorities) take the apostles' teaching as a personal attack: "You are determined to make us guilty". Notice, also, that the high priest doesn't mention Jesus' name, suggesting that the name itself is tainted for him.

Peter's answer (along with "the other apostles") is the same as it was before: "We must obey God rather than human beings!" He then launches into a mini-sermon that covers all the essentials: you killed Jesus "by hanging him on a cross," but the God of your "ancestors" raised Jesus from the dead and "exalted him to his own right hand" so as to "bring Israel to repentance and forgive their sins." Furthermore, they, the apostles, are witnesses of these things together with "the Holy Spirit, whom God has given to those who obey him." These words are infuriating to the religious establishment. Not only is Peter again insisting upon their guilt in Jesus' death, he is suggesting that they repent and ask for forgiveness. Furthermore, by claiming that he and the other apostles "are witnesses of these things," Peter is saying that the authority to teach Israel in the ways of God rests with them, and not with the high priests and Sadducees.

Not surprisingly, these words incite a murderous fury that is calmed by one of their own, the Pharisee Gamaliel (who, not incidentally, was Saul/ Paul's teacher), who urges them to consider the fact that there have been false prophets before whose ministries came to nothing. He points to two, specifically: "Theudas," who "appeared, claiming to be somebody" and had a band of four hundred followers; and "Judas the Galilean," who led a revolt. Both were killed (as Jesus was) but their deaths had the effect of scattering their followers. Gamaliel does not note (but we should!) that the effect of Jesus' death and resurrection stands in utter contrast to this and has been taken as one of the most persuasive evidences of the Resurrection: that the testimony of eyewitnesses to the risen Lord garnered more and more followers, not fewer and fewer, as one would expect for a supposed prophet who remained dead. Gamaliel urges them simply to leave the apostles alone. If their work is purely human, he argues, it will, like the other prophets' work, come to nothing. If it's from God, on the other hand, nothing they do will stop it anyway. Worse, the authorities might discover that they've been fighting against God. We, as readers, know of course that "fighting against God" is precisely what the religious authorities are doing, as do the apostles, who, as in the previous lesson, are determined to fear God rather than humans; to obey God's commands, not human commands.

Though Gamaliel persuades them, they have the apostles flogged and tell them (again!) not to speak in Jesus' name. Remarkably, the apostles leave "rejoicing because they had been counted worthy of suffering disgrace for the Name." Who but the Holy Spirit could engender such boldness? Who but the risen Lord Jesus Christ, seated at the right hand of Israel's God, could inspire such dedication, such that his followers rejoice to partake in his suffering?

Begin by reading aloud:

My children and I enjoy singing a silly song about a cat that keeps coming back even after his owner, who doesn't want him anymore, sends him away again and again. The cat goes away on a ship that sinks, but somehow he survives and comes back. The cat goes up in a hot air balloon miles and miles away, but escapes and comes back, and so on. Nothing stops the cat from finding his way back home, even when it seems very unlikely that he should be able to do so. He is, apparently, an unusually determined cat.

In the last lesson, the religious authorities told Peter and John to stop preaching and healing people in Jesus' name. They didn't think that Peter and John, as ordinary, uneducated men, should be teaching the people of Jerusalem anything about God. That, after all, was *their* job as priests and teachers, and they didn't want Peter and John and the other apostles—whom they took simply to be troublemakers—taking over their job. They were worried that people might start looking up to Peter, John, and the others as the true leaders, instead of looking up to *them*. So they threw them in jail for the night, and released them with a warning not to do any more preaching.

But like that cat who simply could not be gotten rid of, Peter and John are determined to do the work that God has called them to do: to preach about Jesus' death and resurrection, the forgiveness of sins that he offers, and the gift of the Holy Spirit's presence and help. More and more people are following them and coming to believe in Jesus. They are also healing many people who are sick and suffering, and so people are coming to respect and admire them, which makes the high priest and his group—the Sadducees—jealous and angry. They arrest the apostles and have them thrown into jail. You may be thinking, "*Well, surely they won't be able to get out of that!*" And that would be a reasonable thing to think. After all, it's no easy thing to escape from prison, with its bars and locks and guards.

But, like the cat in the silly song who can't be stopped even by a ship-wreck, Peter and John get out of prison and go right back to doing what they were asked not to do: preaching about Jesus in the temple courts! Luke tells us that an "angel of the Lord" opened the door of the jail and told them to "go, stand in the temple courts . . . and tell the people all about this new life." And that's just what they do.

When you lock someone in prison—or when you send a cat away on a ship that later sinks—you feel reasonably sure that you won't be seeing that person or that cat anytime soon. So you can imagine the high priest's surprise the next morning, when he sends for the apostles, only to find that they are not in prison, but are in fact standing in the very place he most wants them to leave, doing the very thing he most wants them to stop doing! The priest's officers bring the apostles before the Sanhedrin so that he may question them. The priest sounds exasperated, saying, "We gave you strict orders not to teach in this name," yet that is what they have gone on doing. He is at least as confused as the man whose cat kept coming back, and as frustrated as grownups are when they say, "How many times do I have to tell you not to leave your wet towel on the floor?" after you've left it on the floor yet again.

Peter's answer doesn't change: he tells the priest yet again, "We must obey God rather than human beings!" Again he tells the priest all the important parts of the Gospel message: Jesus died; God raised Jesus from the dead; Jesus offers forgiveness of sins and the gift of the Holy Spirit. He also says that he and the other apostles are "witnesses of these things," which is another challenge to the priest's authority. Before, the priest might have thought that he and his group knew all there was to know about God, and that they were the only ones who should teach others about God and God's ways. But now the authority to teach the

Lesson 9: Prison Doors Open

truth about God and about God's son, Jesus, has moved from them to this group of uneducated, poor men.

The priest is so angry that he wants Peter and John killed, but a man named Gamaliel, who is also a teacher of the law, calms him. Gamaliel points out that if the apostles are spreading false teaching, it will all eventually come to nothing, but that if their teaching is from God, fighting against them won't do any good anyway. "Leave them alone," advises Gamaliel. "Just wait and see what happens."

The priest takes Gamaliel's advice. He doesn't have the apostles killed, but he has them beaten, and sends them away warning them *again* not to speak about Jesus.

Do you think that the apostles will follow the priest's order, since they've been jailed and beaten for continuing to speak about Jesus?

No! Instead, Luke tells us, they were actually *rejoicing* because they had the chance to suffer because of teaching about Jesus.

The silly song about the cat is just that: a silly song, and certainly not based on a true story. But the apostles' remarkable determination to continue teaching about Jesus and healing people in Jesus' name is surprising, but true.

The Holy Spirit makes them strong, brave, and dedicated to the work that God has given them to do. No prison bars can hold them; no beatings can discourage them; no warning will stop them.

Lesson 10

Acts 6:1-8:3

The Story of Stephen

What the Parent Should Know: Stephen is an important figure in the book of Acts, chosen by the apostles from among the community of Christ-following disciples to oversee the charitable distribution of food to the widows and (presumably) other people in need. This was an important aspect of the ministry of the early church, along with prayer and preaching and teaching, but it appears that the apostles were not able to keep up with all the work to which they'd been called. So they selected seven men "of good standing, full of the Spirit and of wisdom," to undertake that responsibility while they devoted themselves to "prayer and to serving the word." It doesn't appear, however, that Stephen's ministry was limited to simply "waiting on tables;" he is said to be "full of grace and power" and to have performed "great wonders and signs" among the people, which, not surprisingly, attracts the disapproving attention of those in other religious sects, and, finally, of the religious authorities, who accuse Stephen of blasphemy against "Moses and God."

Stephen's speech following his accusation—the longest sermon in the book of Acts (ch. 7)—is an indirect but brilliant response to the charges put to him. In a long historical review, Stephen indicts the religious authorities by showing how they correspond to those who have always wrongly judged, mistreated, and ignored God's prophets. Indeed, before Stephen even begins to speak—when he is accused of claiming that "Jesus of Nazareth will destroy [the temple] and will change the customs that Moses handed on to us" (v. 14)—he is described in distinctly prophet-like terms; his face "was like the face of an angel," which is probably an allusion to the shining appearance of Moses' face after speaking with God on Sinai. The authorities accuse Stephen of blaspheming Moses; Luke means to cast him as a prophet in the tradition of Moses, and the authorities as those who have always opposed God's work in the world.

A significant theme of Stephen's speech is in response to the council's accusation that Stephen and other followers of Jesus mean to destroy the temple—the symbolic center of Jewish religious authority. By telling the story of Israel's history in such a way as to highlight God's work among different people in different places—Abraham, who was called to leave his country and who was promised a portion of land for his "descendants after him," but who never himself set food in the land; Joseph, who was sold by his brothers into slavery in Egypt, where he became the agent of salvation for his family during a great famine; and Moses, who was sent by God to help deliver God's people from bondage to the Egyptians, and who, nonetheless, was rejected by God's people as a ruler. Stephen continues the narrative until, finally, Solomon builds the temple, which, however, is not the final and permanent dwelling place of God, for, as Stephen quotes from Isaiah 66:1, " 'Heaven is my throne, and the earth is my footstool. What kind of house will you build for me?' says the Lord." (Acts 7:49) Stephen's point is that God's promises to bless all the earth through Abraham is not tied to a particular place "made by human hands" (the temple), because all the created order (heaven and earth) is God's temple. Moreover, God's people have consistently rejected God's leaders and prophets, and the present religious authorities are no exception. Stephen calls them a "stiff-necked people, uncircumcised in heart and ears," using a favorite prophetic imprecation (see, for example, Jeremiah 6:10) which draws attention to the fact that while the authorities might have the outward trappings of righteousness, they are unchanged inwardly; unwilling truly to hear the Word of God: "You are forever opposing the Holy Spirit, just as your ancestors did." They believed themselves to be on the side of their ancestor Moses, and Stephen to be the opposition; Stephen argues the reverse, finishing by saying that they have in fact killed the Righteous One of God.

At this point, the religious leaders are furious, and in the face of their anger, Stephen looks into heaven, "filled with the Holy Spirit," and declares that he sees the "glory of God and Jesus standing at the right hand of God." At this, which they take as egregious blasphemy, the council rushes to drive him out of the city, where they stone him to death. His dying words, not incidentally, are very like Jesus': He cries out, "Jesus, receive my spirit" and "Lord, do not hold this sin against them." That Stephen's cries are addressed to Jesus, while Jesus' similar cries were addressed to God the Father, is further testimony that Jesus is in fact one with God the Father.

This story draws what scholars call "the Jerusalem narrative" to a close; the stoning of Stephen begins "a severe persecution" of the church in Jerusalem, and "all except the apostles were scattered throughout the countryside of Judea and Samaria." If we can recall that Jesus' charge to the apostles in Acts 1 was that they should be his witnesses in Jerusalem, Judea, and Samaria, and then to the uttermost parts of the earth, we can see that in God's unexpected and often shocking way, the death of Stephen furthers the growth of the church.

Begin by reading aloud:

Even today, when a church is small, one person, or a small group of people, do many of the different kinds of jobs that are necessary to keep the church's work going. When I was young, my father was the pastor of our little church. He did a lot of different kinds of work: preaching and teaching God's word, of course, and praying for hours for the people in the congregation and in the community. And he visited the people who were too sick or too old to leave their houses and come to church, bringing them communion and gifts of money or food that the church wanted to share with them. Often, my father cleaned the church along with other members of the church. Many times I would help him clean, or to fold bulletins and other papers that announced what was going on in the life of the church that week.

But as the church grew and grew—as more and more people came to believe in Jesus and be baptized and join the life of the church, and as some of those people began to have more and more children—my father and his few helpers couldn't manage to do everything they had done before. There were too many people to be visited and too many people with serious questions about God for just a few people to take care of everything and keep the church clean and bulletins printed and folded and babies looked after in the nursery and so on. So other helpers were chosen from among the people in the church, each to take on different jobs, all of which were very important and necessary in their own ways. Teaching and preaching God's word is important, but so is taking care of people who are sick and old, and so is caring for the babies and young children in church.

The story of Stephen, which has a terribly sad ending, begins just at the point when the group of people in Jerusalem who followed Jesus' teachings was getting large enough that the twelve apostles needed other helpers in order to continue with the work that Jesus had given them to do. Some of the widows—women whose husbands had died, and who may not have been able to earn a living on their own—seemed not to be getting enough food, and distributing food each day was an important part of the church's work. So seven helpers, Stephen among them, were given the job of seeing that the food was being given out fairly. From the way Luke tells the story, it's clear that this work was just as important in the life of the church as the other kind of work. Stephen, it seems, not only distributed food, but also spoke with wisdom and did "great wonders and signs" among the people.

Well, you might be able to imagine what happened next: the religious authorities, those same people who put Peter and John in prison, were not at all happy with Stephen. They said that he was speaking against Moses and God, which was a serious accusation indeed. They were certain he was teaching that the temple itself—the place where the religious authorities exercised their rule—was going to be destroyed by Jesus, and that the "customs" given to them by Moses were going to be changed. They were very sure that Stephen was very wrong, and they wanted him punished.

But when Stephen begins to speak—and he speaks for a long, long time—he tells stories from the history of God's people, Israel, making it clear that God's work has never been limited to one particular place, such as the temple. The whole universe, heaven and earth, is God's temple, and nothing made by human hands can contain God. Furthermore, there have always been people who opposed God's work in the world, who refused to listen to the prophets that God sent to speak God's own messages to the people. The people whom Moses led out of slavery in Egypt turned against him and didn't want to listen to his teaching from

God. Far from speaking *against* Moses, Luke, the storyteller, wants us to see how Stephen is in fact very much *like* Moses. He is faithfully giving the same teaching given him by the apostles who were taught by Jesus Christ. Luke tells us that Stephen's face was shining as he spoke to the religious authorities, just as Moses' face had shone after Moses met with God on Mount Sinai. In so many words, Stephen is saying: "*I'm* not the one working against God and against our religious tradition! *You* are the ones who are refusing to listen to God's messengers, just as people in our history have always opposed God's work and the words of God's messengers, and that's just what you've done by killing Jesus!"

These are not words that the authorities want to hear. Remember, they believe that because of their heritage—the families that they'd been born into—and because of their position as teachers and leaders in the temple, they have a special understanding of what God is doing. They look upon Stephen and all the rest of the Jesus-followers as dangerously misinformed, and, as before, they become very angry and rush at Stephen, and kill him by throwing stones at him until he dies. As he is dying, Stephen prays to Jesus, and his prayer sounds very much like Jesus' prayer to God the Father as Jesus was dying on the cross: Stephen asks Jesus to take his spirit, and he also asks that Jesus forgive the people who are killing him.

Now, of course, those people living in Jerusalem who are following the way of Jesus become very scared, because religious authorities and teachers—including one young man named Saul, about whom we'll learn more later—are now attacking (or "persecuting") those who believe in Jesus. Many of those who follow Jesus are scattered into Judea and Samaria. And strange as it may seem, they are, by scattering (and then "proclaiming the word" wherever they go, (8:4) obeying what Jesus has commanded them: that they should be his witnesses not only in Jerusalem but also in Judea and Samaria.

Stephen's story shows us that Jesus' work in the world is continuing, not only through the twelve apostles, but through other helpers, and through the believers themselves, who shared the teaching about Jesus and the work of Jesus' kingdom wherever they went.

Acts 16:16-40
Conflicts with the Culture and
Setting All Kinds of Captives Free:
Paul and Silas in Prison

What the Parent Should Know: In this episode, which takes place in Philippi, a "leading city of the district of Macedonia and a Roman colony," we begin to see the Gospel of Jesus Christ spread further among Gentiles, towards conflict with the prevailing culture. The careful reader will notice that there appears to be no synagogue from which Paul and Silas can begin to teach, as has been their practice thus far, which is probably simply because there are not enough Jews in that region to form one. As it has been Paul's tendency to begin teaching from places already observant, he and Silas head to Philippi's "place of prayer," meaning, we can assume, a place of pagan worship.

Along the way, a slave girl with a spirit of divination begins to follow them, announcing loudly "these men are slaves of the Most High God, who proclaim to you a way of salvation." Some commentators and preachers have made much of this statement, saying that even though the girl, being possessed, can't be trusted as a source of sound doctrine, what she proclaims is true. However, other commentators, including N.T. Wright and Ben Witherington, have persuasively argued that she is not referring to the God of Abraham, Isaac, and Jacob, but perhaps to Zeus or else another god in the Greco-Roman pantheon.

Apparently Paul and Silas tolerated being tailed by this girl for some time, for verse 18 tells us that "after many days," Paul began to be annoyed and, in the name of Jesus, cast out the shrieking demon, which initiated the conflict with the Roman authorities. The slave girl's owners were angry with Paul, for they had been exploiting her demon-possessed state by charging people for something like fortune-telling. The exorcism was for them the elimination of a source of income. In appealing to the authorities, however, the owners portrayed Paul and Silas as lawbreakers and enemies to Roman culture, as in a sense they were, since there is nothing very Roman about shutting down a fortune-telling operation. Paul and Silas were stripped, beaten, and securely jailed, their feet placed in stocks.

Again these believers exemplify that surprising quality of being joyful while under persecution: singing hymns and praying to God even while they were enchained. The text tells us that the other prisoners were listening, and from this we may surmise that their faithfulness in praising God despite their unfortunate circumstances served as a witness to their profound commitment to the way of Jesus.

In the middle of the night, a violent earthquake occurs. Occasionally earthquakes in the Bible are a sign of God's judgment, but it may be that this earthquake is simply a sign of God's moving—of God doing what God does in Christ: setting captives free. (This is the third time in Acts that God miraculously opens prison doors; it also happens in 5:19 and 12:6-11.) Because his is a culture of honor and shame, the jailer, awakening and seeing that the doors are open, prepares to take his own life. There is irony here: the jailer finds himself impossibly ensnared by the unshackling of the inmates under his care. Understanding this, Paul urges him not to harm himself; they are all still there. Why are they all there? Perhaps because whether he is in prison or out of prison, Paul's aim is to preach the Gospel. Perhaps he senses that voluntarily confining himself to the place to which he had been consigned would stand as testimony for the unusual message he is preaching.

And perhaps it is this extraordinary peacefulness that prompts the bewildered jailer to inquire of them what he must do to be saved—not in terms of how he might be saved eternally, but rather, how he might get out of the situation that he is in. Paul's answer is farther-reaching than the jailer's question: "Believe in The Lord Jesus Christ and you shall be saved; you and your entire household." Following this, the jailer exhibits profound hospitality and solicitude by bringing Paul and Silas home to wash their wounds; they, in turn, baptize him and his family, and together all enjoy the fellowship of the table: once again a picture of the kingdom feast of God, with those who were at enmity and of different ethnic backgrounds sharing a common table.

Finally, the Roman authorities want to conceal the whole odd affair by ushering Paul and Silas away quietly—in contrast to how they entered Philippi, with the shouting of the slave girl. But Paul will have none of that. He will not go quietly. He is, he says, a Roman citizen, and to be beaten and jailed without trial is a violation of his rights. Why does he choose to raise a ruckus instead of leaving quietly? It seems the only explanation that makes sense is that they felt it was important for the sake of the Gospel. It is not for the defense of their own rights that they choose to demand acknowledgment, but so that it might be known more widely that they were willing in the first place—though they might have avoided it by speaking up about their rights as Romans—to be beaten and chained for the God who sets captives free and beckons all people, those in chains and those who snare others in chains, to believe in Jesus and to be saved.

Begin by reading aloud:

This story begins with the Apostle Paul getting annoyed because a girl was following them around the city of Philippi yelling about what they were doing, and it ends with Paul not wanting to leave Philippi quietly, but wanting everyone to know what had happened to them there.

Why was the girl yelling? She was yelling because she was possessed by something called a spirit of divination, which means that she was probably more than just a little strange and disturbed, and also that she had an unusual ability to understand things that were going on around her, and maybe even predict things that were going to happen.

She was a slave girl, and because she was able to tell people about things that were going to happen, or about things that were going on elsewhere, her owners charged people money in exchange for her telling them things. To be possessed as this girl was is a terrible thing. But her owners were using it to make money.

When Paul and Silas came to the city of Philippi, the girl began to follow them, screaming that they were servants of the Most High God, who proclaimed a way of salvation. Now it may be that the girl did understand that Paul and Silas were working for God. But she did not understand about Jesus. Finally, when Paul had enough of her screaming, he commanded the spirit of divination to come out of her, and it did.

We can imagine that she felt relieved when Paul did this. To be acting and speaking in a way that is not quite under your control is a very unpleasant thing. It was deeply kind of Paul to restore her to her right mind.

But no matter how the girl felt, her owners were furious. They had been using her ability to tell the future as a way to make money. Now that she was no longer possessed, they would no longer be able to charge people money in exchange for her telling the future. So they wanted to punish Paul and Silas for this.

The girl's owners went to the authorities—something like the Roman police—and told them that Paul and Silas were disobeying the law and also that they were opposing the Roman way of life. Without finding out whether these accusations were true or not, the authorities had Paul and Silas stripped and thrown into jail with their feet securely bound up in stocks.

Did Paul and Silas begin screaming about how unfair it all was, and how they should not be in jail, and so on? They did not. Instead, they prayed and sang hymns to God. How unusual this must have seemed to the people in jail with them! Here they were in jail without having done

Lesson 11: Conflicts with the Culture

anything wrong, and yet, instead of complaining about it, they were singing and praying to God.

Then, in the middle of the night, there was a violent earthquake that opened the prison doors and loosened Paul and Silas' chains. When the jailer awakened and saw that the doors were open, he was terrified. If the prisoners were gone, he would be in terrible trouble. And surely they must be gone, he thought. After all, if you were in prison for doing nothing wrong at all and the doors suddenly flew open and the prison guard was asleep, you would probably leave.

And the prison guard was so worried about this that he thought the only good choice he had was to end his life.

But Paul and Silas didn't leave. They told the prison guard not to harm himself.

And then, perhaps sensing that these were very unusual prisoners, the guard asked them, "What must I do to be saved?"

"Believe in The Lord Jesus Christ and you shall be saved; you and your entire household," Paul told him.

The jailer brought Paul and Silas home. He washed their wounds. They baptized him and his family. Together, they enjoyed a meal, no longer strangers and enemies, but friends.

At some point, the Roman authorities wanted to cover up this whole strange series of events—the arrest, the beating, the shackling, the earthquake, and the freeing of the prisoners—by having Paul and Silas leave the city of Philippi quietly. But if Paul and Silas wanted the girl to quit shouting about them at the beginning of the story, here at the end they refused to go quietly. It was against the law to beat and imprison a Roman citizen (and Paul was a Roman citizen) without first finding out if the charges against him were true. The authorities had broken the law, and Paul wanted an apology.

Why didn't Paul just leave, quietly? It was because he and Silas wanted more and more people to know what had happened to them, to know that they were willing to be beaten and chained for the sake of preaching about Jesus.

Because, after all, in Jesus, God is welcoming all people—those who are in prison and those who keep others in prison—to come to him and be saved, be baptized, and share a common feast.

How Can Trials Be a *Joy?*

What The Parent Should Know: James' epistle is a letter "to the twelve tribes in the Dispersion," and some commentators note that Acts 8:1 might offer background to this greeting: "That day a severe persecution began against the church in Jerusalem, and all except the apostles were scattered throughout the countryside of Judea and Samaria." With its link to the geographical structure of Acts, this verse seems to suggest that the Gospel's movement "to the ends of the earth" will be driven, at least in part, by persecution. Indeed, that the apostles "rejoice" because they are "considered worthy to suffer dishonor for the sake of the name"(Acts 5:41)—and the overall movement of the narrative of Acts—indicates that they understand on some level what Tertullian would later proclaim: that "the blood of the martyrs is the seed of the church," or, indeed, that they have truly understood the meaning of Jesus' suffering, death, and resurrection, and that their role in the continuing story of God's people is to suffer as Jesus did, for the sake of his name. The people that James is addressing, then, may be people who face "dispersion" for the sake of Jesus.

However, the very general nature of James' greeting leads commentators to suggest that the epistle was not composed with a particular community in mind, but instead that it was (and is!) intended for Christians in every place. Implied in the very idea of dispersion or Diaspora is displacement and, therefore, loss, which is likely why James opens the letter saying, "My brothers and sisters, whenever you face trials of any kind, consider it nothing but joy, because you know that the testing of your faith produces endurance." This instruction strikes us, as it likely struck the original hearers, as profoundly unnatural—the opposite of normal human inclination. Why should suffering be greeted with joy? It is because suffering offers the sufferer an opportunity for the "testing of faith" and the possibility that this testing will produce "endurance," maturity, and completeness.

The counterintuitive nature of James' instruction continues throughout the first chapter, which scholar Luke Timothy Johnson notes serves as an index to topics that later chapters treat in greater detail. For example, the theme of enduring trials (1:2-4; and 12-15) is expanded in 5:7-11, while the point that "doing"—and not just "hearing" the word is introduced in 1:22-26 and developed in 2:14-26). Throughout the first chapter, and, indeed, throughout *the book, James' understanding of God is as a gracious and generous God: God "gives [wisdom] to all generously" and God is the giver of "every perfect gift." God's wisdom—God's word—is not an abstracted "belief"—it generates goodness in the lives of those who treasure it. It is this generous, generative God that James' audience is invited to listen to; this God who will give wisdom to anyone who asks, who will give the "crown of life" to "those who love him." It's this wisdom that makes possible what ordinary human understanding regards as impossible: rejoicing in trials, boasting in poverty (v. 10), enduring temptation (v.12), being "quick to listen, slow to speak, slow to anger," and doing God's (often difficult) word.*

Trials can be "a joy"—for the apostles and, James says, for anyone— because a good and generous God makes this possible.

Begin by reading aloud:

Have you ever had to move to a new house? Or have you ever been far from home and felt sad because you missed home, and longed to go back to see familiar people and familiar things?

From time to time, and for different reasons, people leave their homes and everything that is familiar. Sometimes people move because they have found a new job in a place that's far away. But sometimes, people have to leave their home and the land where they've always lived because war or persecution has made it impossible to stay. That is what happened to the early Christians, some of whom we have already learned about. When people became angry with them, and even violent toward them, many early Christians left their homes and moved elsewhere. Just after Stephen was killed, Luke tells us that "a severe persecution began against the church in Jerusalem, and all except the apostles were scattered throughout the countryside of Judea and Samaria." (8:1) We sometimes call this scattering of people outside their home area "diaspora" or "dispersion." To "disperse" something is to spread it over a wide area. And that is what happened to many early Christians: they were spread out over a wide area.

If you were to scatter a certain kind of wildflower seed outside of your garden, sprinkling these seeds over the dirt along sidewalks and in parks, and they were to grow, they would create more seeds, which would make more flowers, which would create more seeds, and so on. And then a bird might take some seeds and carry them even farther, and the seeds that you scattered would make many, many more flowers farther and farther from your garden. More people would see those flowers than would ever have visited your garden.

The scattering of the Christians throughout Judea and Samaria is something like that. At the beginning of the book of Acts, Jesus asks the apostles to take his teaching "to Judea and Samaria, and to the ends of the earth." Strangely enough, even bad things, like persecution, are helping the seeds of Jesus' teaching to move farther and farther into the world. As Christians were scattered farther and farther from Jerusalem, apostles such as Paul continued to visit them in order to teach and encourage them to keep following Jesus' teaching. But when they were not able to visit, they sent letters.

One such letter is from James, and it is written to "the twelve tribes in the Dispersion," that is, those Christians who have been scattered, most likely by persecution. But in a way, this letter is for every Christian in every time and place. After all, there is a sense in which every Christian person is a part of the dispersion—we have learned about Jesus from others who learned about Jesus from others who in turn learned about Jesus from others, and so on, reaching all the way back to the early Christians and to Jesus himself, just as a wildflower seed carried by a bird far from your garden originated with one of the seeds you first scattered along the sidewalk. And sometimes the way in which Jesus asks us to live seem strange, as if we are not quite at home in this world.

James knows that it is hard to leave home where everything is familiar. But he also knows a very strange truth: that God can transform even suffering into good, just as he did in raising Jesus from the dead. So his letter encourages the Christians to face even difficult times with joy, knowing that if their faith is tested, it will become even stronger, just as your muscles become stronger if you use them. James encourages them to ask God for wisdom, and assures them that God is glad to give wisdom to those who ask for it. It is God's wisdom that makes it possible to understand even teaching that seems very strange, like "consider it nothing but joy" when "you face trials of any kind." James assures his readers that God is a good and generous God. Though God asks difficult things of his children, he also gives them the wisdom to understand those things and a blessing when they do them (v. 25).

Most often we don't (and can't) know what "good" God might be bringing out of trials. Having to leave your home and move to a new place because of persecution is a trial, and the early Christians who faced that trial may not have understood that their dispersion was helping to spread Jesus' message. Nevertheless, that is exactly what happened.

We can't know what the "good" result may end up being, but we can trust that God is good, that God is generous, and that it is God, as James says, who gives us "every perfect gift." By trusting in this good and generous God, we can, James says, face trials with joy.

Lesson 12: How Can Trials Be a *Joy?*

Unit 4

Being a New Creation in Christ

Most stories of conversion to Christianity come nowhere close to the drama and intensity of Paul's Damascus Road experience. Sometimes, a person's experience of being saved is less a "conversion" and more of a gradual recognition, as in this unit's story of the Ethiopian eunuch. Nonetheless, the New Testament consistently speaks of salvation in Jesus as conversion, "new creation," or being "born again." This does not mean that a person's substance—who he or she is—changes when he or she comes to believe in Jesus. Instead it indicates that the believer's priorities, preoccupations, and attitudes toward God and other people have been significantly altered; reoriented to center on Jesus Christ, often with surprising results.

<table>
<tr><td>**Lesson**
13</td><td>**Acts 8:26-40**

An Outsider is Welcomed In</td></tr>
</table>

What the Parent Should Know: In this passage, Philip—one of the seven chosen and blessed by the apostles to serve in Acts 6:1-8—shares the good news of Jesus Christ with a man who is an outsider three times—not only is he not Jewish, he is an Ethiopian man from the queen's court, and he is a eunuch. Nevertheless, Luke tells us, he had come to Jerusalem to worship. Though Philip is a helper and not an apostle, the Holy Spirit as well as "an angel of the Lord" minister to the man through Philip, offering something of a foretaste of the more general welcome to be made to Gentiles later on. Tradition (including the church father, Irenaeus) tells us that this apparently influential Ethiopian man, who, we are told, had charge of the entire treasury of the queen, was responsible for evangelizing his home country, which, commentators say, was not exactly where modern-day Ethiopia is, but, more likely, the ancient kingdom of Nubia which was located near modern-day Sudan.

When the angel of the Lord tells Philip to go down from Jerusalem, we should notice that the Gospel appears to be spreading just as Jesus declared that it should—in Jerusalem, Judea, and Samaria (8:1-25), and now to the uttermost parts of the world, as in Acts 1:8. As a number of commentators (including Ben Witherington and Robert Tannehill) have noted, ancient Near Eastern literature makes clear that Ethiopia was considered to be part of the remotest regions of the known world. Philip, at the prompting of the angel and the Spirit (8:29) goes to him on his way and joins him in his chariot, where he finds the man reading the prophet Isaiah (likely, aloud, as reading silently was rare in the ancient world). "Do you understand what you are reading?" he asks. "How can I, unless someone guides me?" the eunuch says, inviting Philip to sit beside him.

The eunuch is reading from Isaiah 53:

> Like a sheep he was led to the slaughter, and like a lamb silent before his shearer, so he does not open his mouth. In his humiliation justice was denied him. Who can describe his generation? For his life is taken away from the earth.

New Testament scholar N.T. Wright reminds us that the early church read the Old Testament as a great narrative; there was no question of simply linking Old Testament passages up with Jesus. Rather, Isaiah's "suffering servant" passage envisions a man who will take up the work that Israel was meant to do, who will die, bearing all the evil of the world. The subsequent passages in Isaiah envision a new covenant (ch. 53), a new creation (ch. 55), and, significantly for our purposes here, a hospitable welcome to those outside of Israel (ch. 56), which is especially relevant to the Acts passage because eunuchs are specifically included in God's welcome. Castrated men had been specifically forbidden (in Deuteronomy 23:1) from participation in the assembly of the Lord. Here, as throughout the Gospels, Jesus' welcome is *unexpectedly inclusive indeed. Surely this is a major part of the "good news about Jesus" that Philip speaks to the Ethiopian man.*

The Ethiopian man is deeply receptive to Philip's teaching; indeed, he seems to be waiting to hear what Philip has to say, and it is he who points out the water and asks to be baptized. Meanwhile, Luke subtly sketches Philip's ministry as parallel to Jesus'; the lamb before its shearer does not open its mouth; Philip opens his mouth to speak about the scripture. Jesus' life is taken away from the earth; in this passage, the Holy Spirit snatches Philip away and moves him onward, away from Jerusalem.

The Holy Spirit does a mighty work through Philip, and it looks like outsiders being welcomed in and the Gospel of Jesus Christ going to the edges of the world.

Begin by reading aloud:

Have you ever felt like an outsider? Maybe you have been at gatherings where you were the only boy among crowds of girls, or the only girl among crowds of boys. Maybe you have been in places where you were the only child in a roomful of adults. Or maybe you have had other, different experiences of feeling like you didn't quite belong.

By now you probably understand that Jesus' teaching is that whoever will come to him, belongs. Although at certain times and in certain places, people believed that God loved them best of all, because they were the best at keeping the rules or because of who their parents and grandparents and great-grandparents were, the truth is that God welcomes whoever will come to him—whoever will come to Jesus.

Do you remember that Jesus told his disciples to be his witnesses in Jerusalem, in Judea and Samaria, and to the "uttermost" parts of the world? Well, that is exactly what is starting to happen in this story: a man who would have seemed to Jesus' friends like the most extreme kind of outsider is welcomed into the family of believers.

The man was from Ethiopia, an African kingdom that historians think was probably closer to where Sudan is on our maps of Africa today. This was about as far away from Jerusalem as most people in Jerusalem could even imagine. He was a man from the queen's court—the person in charge of handling all of the royal wealth. He was also a eunuch, meaning that he was not like most other men and would never get married or have children.

So he was an outsider in more ways than one.

He wasn't Jewish. He was from as far away as anyone had ever heard. He would never get married or have children the way that most other men would.

But he loved God's word and cared enough about God that he traveled all that very, very long way to Jerusalem—the special city of God; the center of where God was doing his most important work in Jesus—in order to worship. Now he was on his way home, but he was still not quite sure he understood about God.

And so, an angel of the Lord tells Philip—one of the apostles' helpers—to go down from Jerusalem so that the good news about Jesus can continue making its way out from the center. As Philip goes on his way, he finds the Ethiopian man riding in his chariot, reading from Isaiah 53; from the part of the Bible we usually call the Old Testament (but which, at the time, was the only part of the Bible anyone had).

"Do you understand what you are reading?" Philip asks the man.

"How can I, unless someone guides me?" the man replies, inviting Philip to sit beside him.

Here is what the man is reading, from Isaiah 53:

> Like a sheep he was led to the slaughter, and like a lamb silent before his shearer, so he does not open his mouth. In his humiliation justice was denied him. Who can describe his generation? For his life is taken away from the earth.

Who was Isaiah the prophet talking about? He was talking about Jesus, of course. Jesus, who would suffer and die to bear all the evil of the world. As Isaiah's book goes on, he speaks about a "new covenant" and a "new creation" in which God will make all the wrongs and hurts of the world right, and will welcome with generous hospitality all the people of the world who will answer his invitation—including those whom people might regard as "outsiders," like the Ethiopian man.

And this is probably a big part of the "good news about Jesus" that Philip speaks to the Ethiopian man: God's welcome is for everyone.

The Ethiopian man seems to be waiting to hear what Philip has to say, and it is he who points out the water and asks to be baptized. Meanwhile, Luke, the storyteller, gives us some hints in the way he tells the story to suggest that Philip's ministry is in some ways like Jesus'; the lamb before its shearer does not open its mouth; Philip opens his mouth to speak about the scripture. Jesus' life is taken away from the earth; in this passage, the Holy Spirit snatches Philip away and moves him onward, away from Jerusalem.

The Holy Spirit does a mighty work through Philip, and it looks like outsiders being welcomed in, and the Gospel of Jesus Christ going to the very edges of the world.

Lesson 13: An Outsider is Welcomed In

Lesson 14

2 Corinthians 5; and 1 Peter 1
Being in Christ,
Being a New Creation

What the Parent Should Know: The term "born-again Christian" has entered the English language as signifying a variety of things: for some people, a "born-again" Christian is the only type of genuine Christian. As Scot McKnight suggests in The King Jesus Gospel, *one of the distinctive contributions of the evangelical movement is its insistence that Christian faith is something to which each individual must make a specific and intentional commitment (as opposed, for example, to considering oneself Christian simply because one's parents and grandparents identify as such). For some, "born-again Christian" indicates that the person has made a conscious conversion from whatever beliefs and commitments he or she may have previously held, toward a new kind of life—a "rebirth"—as a Christian. For some people, "born-again Christian" seems simply to mean "fanatical," but that is a purely social characterization.*

In fact, the concept of rebirth is a significant New Testament concept; one that is crucial to understanding what is meant by "salvation," "being saved," and "conversion." It is perhaps just as accurate, and more helpful, to speak of rebirth as "re-creation." Jesus' resurrection from the dead into an incorruptible, new-creation body is, throughout the New Testament, envisioned as a first fruits offering of all that is to come: the restored heavens and earth in which believers will be raised, as Jesus has been raised, into bodies that will no longer be subject to death and decay. If anyone is in Christ, Paul writes in 2 Corinthians 5, he or she is a new creation—participating already in the New Creation that is to come in its fullness when Jesus returns once again.

It is difficult to make sense of this, especially in light of the fact that at the present time, our bodies ARE fragile and mortal, and we as yet see only glimpses of God's new creation. Where is the justice and peace of the New Creation in its fullness? Where are the fruits of the Spirit in our lives, if we are really and truly in the New Creation and the old has gone?

It is important to consider that the first creation account, in Genesis, is less about assigning a particular form to each created thing and more about assigning it a particular function. To use an analogy from sports, "creation" in the Bible is less about the kind of wood and paint used to build and form the court, or the kind of metal and fiber used for the net. Rather, "creation" is akin to assigning the function to those elements: this is the free-throw line; this is the hoop through which the ball is meant to go.

In their present form our bodies are still subject to the thousands of shocks and frailties our flesh is heir to. We do not yet have our new-Creation bodies. But if we are in Christ, we have been assigned a new function: new priorities, new tasks. We no longer "live for [our]selves but for him who died for [us]." (2 Corinthians 5:15) If we are in Christ, we have been given new assignments, new identities: we are "Christ's ambassadors," making it known that through Christ God wants all people to "be reconciled to God." (2 Corinthians 5:17-20)

In 1 Peter, the Apostle Peter speaks on a similar theme: Having been given a "new birth into a living hope through the resurrection of Jesus Christ from the dead, and into an inheritance that can never perish, spoil, or fade" (1 Peter 1:3-4), believers in Christ have been born into a new set of priorities. They can be joyful even though they suffer. They can give up comforts for the sake of others. They can say "no" to their selfish and evil desires. In short, they can love others deeply and sincerely, because through being "born again," they have been born into a whole different kind of life and set of priorities (1 Peter 1:23). No longer do they live for the momentary and fleeting pleasures of this life, but they now live in light of the "living and enduring Word of God."

So the concept of the "born-again Christian" is much more than sociological or cultural, signifying instead a transformation in how we are to function in this world: as people who have been born into the promises of the New Creation, and who, as a result, have a whole set of new priorities. Rather than indulging in excess, greed, hedonism, and arrogance, we have been given a new function, to leave behind all the old sins of our flesh and to live as new people, living in light of the priorities of God's New Creation.

Being By Reading Aloud:

Have you ever had the chance to see, or even hold, a very, very new baby? It is an amazing thing to experience. An entirely new person, right there! Who will he turn out to be? What will she love and laugh about? What will he spend his life working on?

You may have heard people talk about "born-again Christians." That phrase means different things to different people, of course, but it helps us to understand something important about what the New Testament writers were trying to tell us when they talked about what it means to be "in Christ" or to be "saved."

Think about that phrase: "born again." Now, as one person in the New Testament was brave enough to point out, it isn't actually possible

Lesson 14: Being in Christ, Being a New Creation

to be born again in the ordinary way that we are all born the first time around. So the New Testament writers must mean something very different when they talk about being "born again."

What they mean is that when a person begins to follow Jesus, he or she begins to act in the world in a very different way than they did before. Another important way that the New Testament writers talk about following Jesus—or "being saved"—is that when a person begins to follow Jesus, he or she is a "new creation."

Well, what does THAT mean? Let's think for a moment about the "old" creation; the first creation in Genesis, when God made the world and everything in it and gave everything and everyone their specific jobs to do. Over and over again, people didn't do so well at the jobs God had given them.

But when Jesus came, he did everything right. He took care of people that others didn't want to have anything to do with. He fed hungry people. He showed people what God's love is like. And when he died, he rose again in a body that will never, ever die. So Jesus shows us what the New Creation is like: the New Creation means no more death or sadness or unfairness. It means generosity, kindness, and sharing.

And so when the New Testament writers say that those who believe in Jesus have been "born again" or are "new creations," they are thinking about how Jesus has already begun living that New Creation life.

This is hard for us to understand. Right now, we don't see God's new creation very clearly, at least not most of the time. People still get sick, pets that we love still die. Sad, awful, and unfair things still happen quite often.

But if we are following Jesus, Paul and the other New Testament writers tell us, we have the promise that things will not always be that way. We have new kinds of jobs to do. Certain things are now much more important than anything else. No longer should we be thinking only about ourselves and the things we most want. No longer should we be greedy and envious and competitive. Instead, we can live as if we are already a part of God's New Creation—because, in fact, we are. We can tell other people that God wants to welcome them into the New Creation as well. We can help comfort people who are hurting and share what we have.

And we can be joyful even though bad things happen to us, because we know that these bad things are not going to be the end of the story, any more than Jesus' death was the end of the story, since he rose again from the dead into a body that would never again die. If we follow Jesus, the bad things that happen to us are not the end of the story.

In so many ways, we may seem to be exactly the same people we always were, even after we start to follow Jesus. We are not "born again" like a brand-new baby, but we are "born again" and "new creations" because our way of being in the world has changed. What we love and what we do has changed. Instead of living selfishly, worried mostly about our own things, when we follow Jesus, we leave behind those things and live as members of the New Creation that God is already making: a world of peacefulness, sharing, kindness, and fairness.

Unit 5

Who is Paul?

Though not one of the original twelve apostles, having come to faith in Jesus only after a blinding vision stopped him in his murderous tracks, the Apostle Paul is a figure of incalculable influence in the history of Christianity. A student of the Torah, Paul went on to pen many of the books that make up the New Testament, explaining the significance of Mosaic Law and the supremacy of Jesus Christ in fulfilling that law, and arguing that faith in Jesus, not adherence to things like dietary rules and circumcision, was what allowed people to be declared righteous before God. Though Paul's reputation seems largely built on his rigorous (and significant) theological contributions, the spirit of his epistles is also deeply pastoral; by turns affectionate and tender, and at times stern, even harsh. Even so, his deep concern for the churches under his care and his joyful passion for the Gospel of Jesus Christ always come through.

Lesson	Acts 9:1-9
15	From Enemy to Brother: The Conversion of Saul

What the Parent Should Know: Saul's dramatic conversion—from a highly educated fire-breathing persecutor of the church to passionate apostle of Jesus

Christ—is well-known within Christendom. The "Damascus Road experience" has become a kind of shorthand for unexpected, drastic turnarounds; when spiritual experiences come in suddenly or mystically or in a flash of insight: Augustine hears a voice urging him to take up the Scriptures and read; young Martin Luther fears for his soul and cries out to God; a hardened criminal breaks down, sensing the presence and mercy of Jesus. So dramatic is Saul's conversion that he, like Abraham, is given a new name (Paul) showing that he has been made new in Christ, with a new identity and calling.

Luke begins the conversion narrative by telling us that Saul was "still breathing out murderous threats against the Lord's disciples." In the previous story, Luke noted that Saul was looking on approvingly as Stephen was being stoned to death. Saul is on his way to Damascus with letters of recommendation from the high priest so that "if he found any there who belonged to the Way . . . he might take them as prisoners to Jerusalem." Much as the apostles are going out from Jerusalem with the Gospel of Christ, Saul is going out to gather in whatever believers he finds in order to imprison them, and, we may guess, to prevent the further spread of "the Way" (as early Christianity was then known). As he nears Damascus, a light from heaven flashes around and he falls to the ground. A voice says to him, "Saul, Saul, why do you persecute me?"

Saul immediately recognizes the authority—if not the identity—of this voice, for he asks, "Who are you, Lord?"

"I am Jesus, whom you are persecuting," the voice says, a subtle but significant suggestion of Jesus' intimacy with his followers: Saul persecutes them, and it is the same as persecuting Jesus.

"Get up and go into the city," Jesus says to Saul, "and you will be told what you must do."

In an echo of Jonah's three days in the belly of the fish and Jesus' three days in the tomb, Saul experiences three days of blindness, during which he "did not eat or drink anything"—a sign of contrition, perhaps, or shock-induced fasting and prayer.

Meanwhile, Jesus calls a disciple, Ananias, through a vision, to respond to Saul's prayers. "In a vision he [Saul] has seen a man named Ananias come and place his hands on him to restore his sight," The Lord says to him.

Ananias is understandably reluctant to go, having heard of all the dreadful things Saul has been doing in Jerusalem and that he has come to Damascus to further the reach of his persecution. But surprisingly enough, Jesus has other plans. "Go!" he says to Ananias. "This man is my chosen instrument *to proclaim my name"*—not only to the people of Israel, but *"to the Gentiles and their kings."*

It is astonishing how Ananias greets Saul when he enters the house: he puts his hands on him and calls him "brother," that he "may see again and be filled with the Holy Spirit." Immediately Saul's sight is restored, and he is baptized.

This is a surprising conversion on several levels. That God would choose one of the most passionate persecutors of Christians to preach the Gospel of Jesus to Israel and the Gentile world is another indication of God's astonishing hospitality. This story stands as an example of God's unexpected ways: Ananias, like us, can't quite believe what Jesus is asking him to do. Saul is the archenemy of the Way! But Jesus has a way of making enemies into brothers. And that is what happens with Paul.

Begin by reading aloud:

In some tellings of the fairy tale *Beauty and the Beast*, the young man turns into a beast because he is so unkind. Until he can change his ways and learn how to be kind and how to share with others, he will have a scary appearance to match his scary behavior. Other fairy tales and stories have this kind of switch: from villain to hero; from bad guy to good guy. Can you think of some examples?

You know by now that God has a way of doing things in an upside-down, unexpected manner. God chooses the outsiders, the people that no one wants, and the people that others think are foolish or unimportant. In this story, God transforms one of the worst enemies of Jesus' early followers into an apostle of Jesus—one who has seen Jesus, knows Jesus, and teaches others about Jesus.

Just before our story begins, the young man named Stephen was stoned to death for talking about Jesus. And who was there, looking on and thinking that this was exactly what *should* happen to Stephen?

Saul.

Just as Jesus told his apostles to be his witnesses not only in Jerusalem, but also in the whole area and, eventually, throughout the world, so Saul is determined to pursue other followers of "the Way" (that's what people called Christianity before it was given the name "Christianity"), even if he has to travel. So he does travel, to Damascus, with a letter from the high priest giving him permission to arrest any followers of the Way and bring them back, as prisoners, to Jerusalem.

Luke tells us that Saul was breathing out murderous threats—that is, he was so angry with followers of the Way that he wanted to have them killed and was planning to do just that.

But while he is still on the way to Damascus, a blinding light flashes around him and he falls to the ground. A voice from heaven says, "Saul, Saul, why do you persecute me?"

"Who are you?" Saul asks.

"I am Jesus, whom you are persecuting."

When Saul harms Jesus' followers, he is also harming Jesus. And so Jesus is having a word with Saul.

"Get up and go into the city," Jesus says to him, "and you will be told what you must do."

So Saul does just that. For three days, he is blind—unable to see—and does not eat or drink anything. This is a sign that a great change is coming over him. When his eyes are opened, he will be a transformed person.

Meanwhile, Jesus, through a vision (something like a dream), calls upon one of his followers, Ananias, to go to Saul. Saul has had a vision, too, Jesus says, and in Saul's vision, a man named Ananias comes to him, places his hands on him, and restores his sight.

Now, imagine for a moment that you are Ananias. You really would not want to go anywhere near Saul—remember, he is the man who is going around trying to find followers of Jesus so that he can bring them to Jerusalem and, he hopes, have them killed! Why is Jesus asking Ananias to do this strange thing?

"Go!" Jesus says to Ananias. Saul is going to be an important "instrument" that God will use to tell people about Jesus: not just the people of Israel (of whom Saul was one), but also everyone else.

And so Ananias obeys Jesus and goes. When he goes to where Saul is staying, he puts his hands on him and calls him "brother," asking God to allow Saul to see again and to fill him with the Holy Spirit. Then Saul's eyesight returns, and he is baptized.

Ananias can't quite believe what Jesus is asking him to do. But he does it. And he gets to see an amazing transformation—the transformation of Saul from his worst enemy to his brother.

This is one of the unexpected ways of God. God can make the blind see. God can take the person who hates Jesus most and turn that person into an apostle. God can take enemies and make them brothers.

Philippians 3

What Paul Gave Up

What the Parent Should Know: Why was Paul, before his Damascus Road experience, so determined to destroy the growing community of people who followed Jesus?

He was not motivated by pure hate, though of course his actions were hateful. But we can understand Saul/Paul better when we understand where he was coming from.

Paul was understandably proud of his "particularly impressive Jewish heritage," writes New Testament scholar Luke Timothy Johnson. For Paul was not only born into prominence as a Jew; he also worked diligently to become who he was: a perfect Pharisee.

In Philippians 3:4-6, Paul details some of his reasons for being "confident in the flesh;" that is, for being confident that his own efforts earned him favor before God.

If other people have reasons for being "confident in the flesh," Paul says, he has more. Under the law (Torah), Paul was absolutely righteous, a perfect Torah-follower; as a "Hebrew born of Hebrews," Paul was a Jewish blue blood. He was circumcised on the eighth day, highly educated as a student of the law, and so passionate about the law that he was willing to persecute those he regarded as law-breakers. "As to righteousness under the law," he was "blameless." This should not be understood as empty boasting, but as an accurate description of who Paul was.

Paul was a Pharisee. For him, scrupulous, zealous, detailed law-keeping was of paramount importance. He believed perfect Torah observance to be the way that a person could be righteous before God—and he was really good at it. "I advanced in Judaism beyond many among my people of the same age, for I was far more zealous for the traditions of my ancestors," he writes in Galatians 1:14.

That Paul, as a Jew, was also a Roman citizen by birth (rather than by purchasing his citizenship) indicates that his was also a socially prominent family. Thus we can surmise that Paul's was a life of relative privilege and that he had plenty of good reasons to be proud of who he was—and that he had many reasons to oppose the growing group of Jews who were following

Jesus; that is, those who were declaring a different way of being righteous before God, apart from keeping the Torah.

For Paul to follow Jesus involved giving up a lot. You may remember from the stories in the Gospels (Telling God's Story Year One through Year Three) that Jesus' most passionate opponents were also those who were most passionate about keeping the Torah. If you excel at keeping the law, the last thing that you want to hear is that righteousness before God doesn't depend upon keeping the law, at least not in the way that you thought. You certainly don't want to hear that Jesus, who appears not to keep the law properly at all, is the only way to righteousness before God.

Yet though he had so much to boast in, at least according to the tradition he was born and raised into and loved with a zealous love, Paul eventually came to regard all those things as loss because of "the surpassing value of knowing Christ Jesus my Lord." (Philippians 3:8). Because of his devotion to Jesus, Paul lost all those things that he was so proud of. But he did not pine after them. Rather, he regarded them as rubbish compared to knowing Christ, and was willing to give them all up—and to give up his very life—in order to know Christ more and make him known to others.

Few people could claim what Paul could claim. By the measure of his own community, he was something of a superstar. But he gave it all up, and humbled himself to become a servant of Jesus, much as Jesus had given up all HIS power and privilege as God to become a human being.

Paul was a remarkable person. He had so many good reasons to be proud of who he was, and he gave it all up, recognizing that even his best efforts were rubbish compared with the surpassing value of knowing Jesus.

Begin by reading aloud:

Sometimes when people say they're the best at something, they're speaking sort of wishfully: they WISH that they were the best—the fastest, the smartest, the funniest—but they're not, really, and it would be better for them, and for everyone else, if they would stop bragging about themselves. And anyway, we usually think that it isn't very good manners to talk about yourself as if you are the best.

But sometimes a person has good reason for saying that they are the best at something.

I had a friend who, at one time, was one of the best pianists in the whole world. He won some of the most important and difficult piano competitions, and the best music schools in the world wanted him to play and teach there. He had good reasons for saying that he was one of the best at the piano, because he really was. But as it happened, he almost never spoke of how talented he was. For him, it was more important that he use his musical gifts to help other people—and to serve Jesus. He gave up many chances to be famous and well-known in order to serve Jesus.

The Apostle Paul's story was something like this. We first met Paul when he was furious at the growth of Jesus' followers, and was, in fact, supporting those who were putting Christians like Stephen to death for telling others about Jesus.

This was a terrible thing, of course. But we need to understand who Paul was to understand why he would do such awful things. He was a Pharisee—a person, you may remember, who was very, very good at keeping God's laws. He was born into a family that was well-known and important in his religious community. People would have looked up to them. And Paul himself was very passionate about keeping God's law. He believed that keeping the law perfectly was the most important thing—the way to be righteous before God—and he was really good at keeping the law perfectly. Among his own community, he could be very proud of who he was. He was one of the best.

So it makes sense that he would be angry with the growing group of people who were following Jesus—they were saying that keeping the law perfectly, as he did, wasn't actually the most important thing. The most important thing was not to keep every rule, but to follow Jesus.

Imagine that you believed the only way to be rewarded with a wonderful gift was to keep a certain set of rules perfectly. And so you kept those rules absolutely perfectly—better than anyone else around you. You would feel proud of yourself, and feel certain that you deserved your reward more than other people. And you might well be right.

But then let's say that someone comes along and tells you that you're wrong: keeping the rules absolutely perfectly isn't the only way to be rewarded. Other people who haven't been keeping the rules at all are going to be rewarded, too. You would probably feel annoyed and even angry, just as Paul did. He really was the best at keeping the law. So he certainly didn't want to hear that Jesus, not perfect law-keeping, is the only way to be righteous before God.

When Paul met Jesus, however, he gave up all the things that he was so proud of. All of his very good reasons for being proud, he said, were nothing at all—rubbish, garbage, trash!—compared with knowing Jesus. He was willing to give up everything that he had been so proud of in order to know Jesus and to help others to know Jesus.

Not many people could say they were the best the way Paul could. But he gave it all up to serve Jesus, much like Jesus, who is God, gave up so much of his power and privilege to become a human being like us.

So Paul is a remarkable person. He had many good reasons to be proud, but he gave it all up to know Jesus. And this shows us, also, how remarkable Jesus is.

<table>
<tr><td>**Lesson**
17</td><td align="right">**Acts 17**
Paul, the Idols,
and the Philosophers</td></tr>
</table>

What the Parent Should Know: In this story, Paul is in the Greek city of Athens, which, as he notices with distress, is full of idols. As is typical practice of the other apostles and ministers of the Gospel, Paul goes to the synagogue to talk with Jewish people about Jesus—but he also spends his time in the marketplace, talking with "those who happened to be there." Because there were religious objects everywhere, the opportunity to talk about religious things would have come up everywhere, not just in designated worship spaces. Paul also engages philosophers in debate, an activity that his education as a Pharisee would have well prepared him to undertake.

Apparently, what Paul has to say seems new and interesting to the Greeks, if a bit confusing and odd. Whatever it is, it seems foreign. But, Luke notes, the Athenians all love novelty—listening to and discussing the "latest ideas"—so they want to hear more. The philosophers bring Paul before the Areopagus (the council of city elders) and ask him to explain his ideas further. He uses the opportunity to preach to them.

When speaking with Jewish people, Paul would ordinarily begin talking about Jesus from the Hebrew Scriptures. Here, speaking to Greeks, Paul takes their "idols," the very thing that had "greatly distressed" him as he explored the city, as his starting point for conversation.

"You're very religious in every way," he says. So religious, in fact, that they even have an altar "to an unknown god." Paul seizes upon this bit of zealous pagan worship and tells them about the God who is, indeed, "unknown" to them: the God who made heaven and earth, and who cannot be contained in shrines or idols or buildings built by human hands. Unlike pagan idols and gods, God does not need to be placated and fed and tended by human hands. On the contrary: the true God is the one who made us, giving human beings "life and breath and everything else." And so God, having made human beings, needs nothing from them. Yet despite this self-sufficiency, God is not

aloof, but actively desires that people "seek him and perhaps reach out for him and find him"—he who "is not far from us." Here Paul quotes the Greek poet Aratus to underline his point: "We are his [God's] offspring"—though of course the Greek poet would not have had the God of Abraham, Isaac, and Jacob in mind as he penned those words.

From there, Paul continues his earlier argument: If WE are HIS offspring, we should not think of God as being like anything that can be made by human hands. "We should not think that the divine being is like gold or silver or stone—an image made by human design and skill," Paul says. "In the past God overlooked such ignorance," he says, "but now he commands all people everywhere to repent." For the invisible God has shown people his son, Jesus Christ, who is the true image and likeness of God, unlike the idols around Athens. Though Paul doesn't refer to Jesus by name, he speaks of him—and of his resurrection—as the basis and assurance of God's just judgment that is to come.

While some scoff at Paul, others want to hear more of what he has to say; still others believe right away.

In this story, we see that the Gospel is for all people, and that many things, even false gods, can serve as starting points for discussions and illustrations of truths about God. We also see the typical response to Gospel teaching: some scoff, some believe, and some want to hear more before they can decide what to think.

Begin by reading aloud:

Have you ever felt shy or embarrassed when meeting new people, even meeting other children? It can feel awkward at first, until you start figuring out what things you may have in common, what you can talk about, and how you might play together. You need to find a kind of meeting point—something you can agree to talk about or do together—before you can start to be friends.

When Paul (and other apostles and ministers) wanted to talk with Jewish people about Jesus, they would start by talking about the Hebrew Bible (what we call the Old Testament), because that is something they both understood and could discuss. The story of Jesus is, in so many ways, a continuation of the story of the Old Testament, so by telling the story of Jesus that way, Paul and others made it easier for Jewish people to understand.

But in this story, Paul isn't talking much with Jewish people—he is in Athens, a Greek city, talking with people who mostly follow what we call pagan religions. Their city is full of idols—statues representing different gods. Normally, Paul would go straight to the houses of worship—synagogues—to talk with people about God. And he does that in Athens, too, but it seems that most people gather in the marketplace and city to discuss ideas about religion and life.

After hearing Paul talk a little about God, some of the philosophers—people who spent most of their time thinking and talking about the way things are, and why things are the way they are, and what makes things beautiful or ugly, bad or good, true or false—asked Paul to come to the Areopagus, which was a kind of council of the older, wiser people of the city, and share more of his thoughts on God.

Unlike most Jewish people at that time, these Greek people do not care much at all about what the Hebrew Bible might have to say, and what it might have to do with Jesus. But they do care about their gods, and their statues and monuments to those gods. They care about their religion. So Paul begins to tell them about Jesus—and about the true God—by talking to them first about their own religion.

"I can see that you are very religious people," Paul says. "You even have an altar that says it is dedicated to an unknown god." The Greeks believed in many different gods, and also thought that those gods had to be taken care of and pleased, lest they become angry and harm people or cause crops to fail. By making an altar to an unknown god, they were probably just trying to make sure that they didn't accidentally anger a god that they hadn't known existed.

So Paul takes this "unknown god" as a chance to tell the Athenians about the true God. "You're worshiping an unknown god, so let me explain this God to you," is what he says. The true God is the God who made heaven and earth, and this God can't be made into an idol, or live in a building made by people. This God doesn't need to be appeased with monuments and sacrifices. This God made people—gave us "life and breath and everything else"—and doesn't need anything from us.

Yet even though God does not need anything from us, Paul tells them, he still wants to be near to us; wants people to look for and find him. "We are his children," Paul says, quoting from a Greek poem. We are GOD's children. And if we are HIS children, we shouldn't think of God as being like anything that a person could make—an idol, or a statue made out of gold or silver or stone. Instead, Paul suggests, if we want to see what God is like, we have to look at Jesus.

And even though God has been patient with people who made idols and worshiped false gods in confused ways, now that God has sent Jesus, God wants people everywhere (not just Jewish people, but Greeks and

Romans and everyone else) to see who he truly is, to change their ways, and to follow Jesus.

Some of the people in Athens scoff at Paul. Some of them want him to go on and say more about the true God. And some of them believe in Jesus right away.

In this story, we can see that even false gods can serve as a starting point for a discussion about the true God. We see that the good news about Jesus is for all people. And we see that while some people believe right away, others will scoff and not want to listen, and still others will want to hear more about Jesus.

Unit 6

The Good News is for Everyone!

One of the most scandalous things about Jesus is the radical welcome he offers even to those who seem to be most on the fringes of society. In his earthly ministry he was often scolded and criticized for the kind of company he chose to keep; frequently, in the Gospels, we see him discouraging the religious elites of his day from thinking that their sterling pedigrees alone will save them. He is clear: His call, much like God's in Isaiah 55, is to anyone who is thirsty—to anyone who will come. At times, this openness (and the ramifications it has even for practical matters such as eating and drinking) is difficult even for his disciples to grasp. But grasp it they must, for it is clear: the Gospel is for everyone.

Lesson 18

Acts 10:1-48

Peter Goes to Cornelius' House

What the Parent Should Know: Acts 10 is worth reading in full for the skillful, back-and-forth way in which Luke tells the story. He begins by introducing Cornelius, who is a Gentile and a Roman centurion. Though we don't know exactly how it came to be, Cornelius is, apparently, very devout: he "gave alms generously to the people and prayed constantly to God." (10:2)

He does not seem to know anything about Jesus, but the Holy Spirit is clearly at work, for Cornelius is visited by a vision of an angel of God, who urges him to find "a certain Simon who is called Peter, who is staying with Simon, a tanner." (10:6) Cornelius immediately sends two of his slaves and one of his "devout" soldiers to go and find Peter.

Here the narrative shifts to Peter, who is on the roof of Simon's house, praying. The detail that Simon is "a tanner" is not insignificant. Tanners were, because of their work, "unclean," but the Holy Spirit is moving him toward something even more radical, and the vision he receives is about to prepare him for it. While he is up on the roof, he is hungry. He wants something to eat, but while it is being prepared, he has a very strange vision in which "something like a large sheet" appears to come down from heaven with all kinds of unclean animals in it. A voice from heaven tells him to "kill and eat," and Peter is horrified. "I have never eaten anything that is profane or unclean," he says. The voice from heaven tells him, "What God has made clean, you must not call profane."

What does this strange vision mean? Peter is already staying at the house of "unclean" Jews, but the Holy Spirit is now calling him to go the home of a Gentile—which was, for Peter, almost an unthinkable thing. It was unlawful for Jews to associate with Gentiles, and to eat unclean food was also unlawful, as well as a huge marker of identity. This is nothing exceptional; every culture has its taboos, including food taboos. To eat unclean food is to give up an enormous part of who Peter understands himself to be and to whom he belongs. But it seems that the Holy Spirit is forming a new culture, a new people, and Peter is receptive to the Holy Spirit's prompting, so he leaves for Cornelius' house the next day. Arriving there, says that while "it is unlawful for a Jew to associate with or to visit a Gentile," God has shown him that he "should not call anyone profane or unclean," and that's why he has come right away. "Now may I ask why you sent for me?" he asks.

Listening to Cornelius' reply, Peter realizes that the Holy Spirit has brought him together with Cornelius to bear witness to the risen Jesus, and to proclaim that "everyone who believes in him"—regardless of nationality or ethnicity—"receives forgiveness of sins through his name." Instead of being defined by what they eat or don't eat, what they wear or don't wear, and whom they associate or don't associate with, this new "culture" formed by the Holy Spirit will be defined not by exclusion but by faith in Jesus, and confirmed by the Holy Spirit and baptism with water. As Peter spoke to Cornelius and his household about Jesus, the Holy Spirit came upon them; they were speaking in tongues and praising God. For Peter, this confirms that

Gentiles as well as Jews can receive the Holy Spirit and should *receive baptism by water "in the name of Jesus Christ."*

Faith in Jesus is not just for Jews, but for Gentiles too, and God is calling the disciples to share that news and to embody it in their relations with other people—relationships that cross the boundaries of class and ethnicity to be defined by faith in Jesus and the transformed life that follows from that faith.

Begin by reading aloud:

Have you ever noticed that some movies and books tell stories in a back-and-forth way? In one scene—or in one chapter—you're with a certain set of characters in one place, but instead of continuing that part of the story, the next scene or chapter follows another character or group of characters in another place. It is almost as if two stories run alongside each other on parallel train tracks, and then the two tracks blend into a single one when the characters meet and their separate stories become a single story. It's a way of telling a story that makes it exciting, especially if the two groups are enemies, and they come together to fight—or come together in order to reconcile, to get along.

This chapter in Acts is a bit like that—it's a story that follows two tracks until the tracks meet up, bringing together two groups of people that were thought to be, if not enemies, then certainly *not* friends. It opens with Luke telling us about a man named Cornelius. Cornelius is a Gentile, which simply means that he is not Jewish. At this point in history, Jesus' followers, including his apostles, didn't realize that when Jesus asked them to be his witnesses *everywhere*, he meant that the Gospel, or good news, was for *everyone*. They thought that it was mostly—or even *only*—for Jewish people.

But in the long story of God's people—told throughout the entire Bible—there have always been Gentiles who believed in God, prayed to God, and did the sort of thing that God asks of his people, things like treating people fairly and sharing what you have. Cornelius is this sort of Gentile. We don't know how he came to know God, but Luke tells us that he "gave alms generously to the people and prayed constantly to God." Cornelius doesn't yet know about Jesus, but a vision of an angel of God comes to him, telling him to find "Peter, who is staying with Simon, a tanner." Cornelius listens to the angel, and sends some of his servants to find Peter.

Now the storyteller switches over to tell us Peter's part of the story. Peter is, as the angel told Cornelius, staying with Simon, who is a tanner. A tanner is a person who turns animal skins into leather. It is, as you might imagine, a very smelly and messy job. And according to the laws in the Old Testament—the Bible of Jewish people both then and now—the work that a tanner does makes them "unclean." All kinds of things can make a person "unclean," and different foods, particularly meats, can be either "clean" or "unclean," depending on what kind of animal they came from. Cows and chickens are clean, but shrimp and pigs are not clean. This sort of thing made it difficult for Jewish people to eat with Gentiles, and they came to believe that even being with Gentiles was itself "unclean."

But while Peter is at Simon's house, he goes up on the roof to pray, and while he is praying, he, like Cornelius, has a vision. And what a strange vision it is! "Something like a large sheet" appears to come down from heaven, and in it are all kinds of unclean animals. The voice from heaven tells Peter to get up, kill some animals, and eat them. But that can't be right—these things are *unclean*, Peter protests. And then the voice from heaven tells him, "What God has made clean, you must not call unclean."

What does this mean? Peter was already staying with someone who was a little bit unclean—a Jewish person with an unclean job—but now the Holy Spirit was telling him to go to the home of a person Peter thought of as *very* unclean—a Gentile! But the vision of the unclean animals has taught Peter something: that God has erased those sorts of "clean and unclean" separations and intends for Peter to bring the Gospel to Gentiles, because neither they, nor pigs and shrimp, are unclean. God has made it *all* clean.

The two tracks of the story come together as Cornelius' men find Peter and call him to come to Cornelius' house, which he does right away. Peter even *stays* in Cornelius' house, which means that he must have eaten all kinds of things that he would never have eaten before—because before he would have said, "This is unclean!" But Peter is beginning to understand that God really has made all things clean, and he is beginning to understand that the Gospel is for *everyone*, and not just for Jewish people. As Peter tells Cornelius and his household about Jesus—about his teaching, his death, and his resurrection, and the fact that "everyone who believes in him receives forgiveness of sin through his name," the Holy Spirit comes upon Cornelius and the others listening.

Peter understands now that faith in Jesus is forming a new kind of group. Instead of people being kept separate from each other based on what they eat or don't eat, or who their parents were, or where they were born, the Holy Spirit is forming a new group: one that is formed when people believe in Jesus.

Lesson 19

Acts 15:1-35
What Do *Gentiles* Have
to Do to Be Saved?

What the Parent Should Know: This passage chronicles an important event that is commonly referred to as the Jerusalem Council. The Jerusalem Council addressed the confusion and conflict that arose in the city of Antioch, when people had come down from Judea to teach Gentile believers that in order to truly be saved, they had to be circumcised in keeping with the law of Moses. Circumcision was a practice regarded as unpleasant, to say the least, to most non-Jewish people in that time and place.

In sum, this is a story about one of the earliest theological conundrums of the church: Did Gentile believers have to essentially become Jewish in order to be saved?

When Paul and Barnabas encountered these people—whom Paul will later refer to as "Judaizers" in his letters—they began to debate intensely, before making their way to Jerusalem to seek the opinion of the apostles and elders there. But their own opinion is already evident: as they made their way to Jerusalem, they made it their business to let people know all the ways in which God had been at work among the Gentiles, calling many of them to believe in the Gospel of Jesus Christ, with no circumcision or Mosaic law-keeping in evidence.

Perhaps somewhat predictably, in Jerusalem, believers who were a part of the Pharisee group insisted that Gentile believers had, essentially, to become Jewish in order to become followers of Jesus: they had to be circumcised and had also to keep the law of Moses—the Torah.

After much discussion, Peter begins to speak, boldly testifying to the fact that God specifically chose and called him to bring the Gospel to Gentiles, and that God gave them the Holy Spirit just as he had given it to every other believer, without showing favoritism.

Furthermore, Peter says, why should they put God to the test by burdening Gentiles with "a yoke that neither we nor our ancestors have been able to bear?" Keeping the law has always been hard, and, after all, Peter notes, it is not by keeping the law that anyone is saved. The way of salvation is the same for everyone: it is not through demonstrations of faithfulness to God embodied in law-keeping, it is, rather, through the grace of the Lord Jesus Christ.

Which is to say, now that Jesus has come and fulfilled the law, he has extended the possibility of becoming a part of God's family to ALL people.

Testifying to the sincerity of God's work among the Gentiles, Paul and Barnabas continue to tell about all the signs and wonders God had done through Gentiles.

Then James—probably James, the brother of Jesus—quotes from the Old Testament book of Amos, chapter 9, to explain that the inclusion of Gentiles in the people of God shouldn't come as a surprise or a shock: it is what God has had in mind all the time.

It is then decided that the burden of circumcision and adherence to Mosaic Law should not be placed upon Gentiles. Rather, it is decided that only a few things should be suggested: that Gentile believers abstain from food sacrificed to animals, from meat from strangled animals, from blood, and from sexual immorality.

Some commentators suggest that the dietary laws have to do with facilitating table fellowship between Jewish and Gentile believers, and to help Gentile believers not act in ways that would be needlessly offensive to their Jewish neighbors. Others suggest that the four proscriptions are deeply connected and summed up as follows: "Avoid anything having to do with pagan worship." Food sacrificed to idols is clearly associated with pagan worship; meat from strangled animals and blood were consumed as part of pagan rituals, while sexual immorality, in this context, is likely associated with pagan temple prostitution.

Judas and Silas, who stayed with Gentile believers for a time, delivered this message personally. And the believers found this message encouraging: they were not going to have to start living like law-keeping Jewish people in order to follow Jesus. They could be believers and still maintain something of their own cultural identity, so long as they were not actively following the practices of pagan religions.

The Jerusalem Council suggests several things. First, that there is no place for ethnic and cultural prides and prejudices, since salvation does not come as a result of assiduous law-keeping, but through the grace of Jesus. Second, that cultural differences should be respected so as not to form barriers to fellowship or concessions to idolatrous religious practices; while at the same time, certain accommodations must be made so as not to place unreasonable burdens on people and permit them to retain a measure of their cultural identity.

Begin by reading aloud:

To understand what is going on in this story, you need to understand something that many people today have forgotten: that very, very early on in the life of the church, most of the people who believed in Jesus were Jewish. That is easy to forget, sometimes, because today people think of Christianity as being completely separate from Judaism.

And while they are indeed different religions, in the time just after Jesus returned to heaven, with his disciples and apostles busy sharing the good news of his resurrection, many, many of the people who believed in him believed in him as people who had been born Jewish and grew up worshiping God in the way that God had asked their ancestors years and years and years before to worship, which means that they had all sorts of laws and traditions that were very important to them—things that they had always done to show that they followed God. This was their way of life.

Now, it was always true that people who were not born into a Jewish family could become worshipers of the same God that Jews worshiped. Several of the great-great-great (and so on!) grandmothers of Jesus did not grow up Jewish, but came to know and love the God of the Jews, the God of Israel. That was what God always wanted: God always wanted people from all nations to come and see how Israel worshiped God, so that God could welcome people from every nation to be part of his family.

But now that this is actually happening—now that people who are not Jewish are beginning to believe in Jesus—some of the people are getting a little confused and even starting to argue a little with one another. They think that Gentiles—people who are not Jewish—have to actually become Jewish in some important ways in order to believe in Jesus and be saved. They believed that these Gentiles had to start keeping the same laws—the laws of Moses—that Jewish people kept.

It is a little bit difficult to imagine what this would be like, but perhaps you can understand what it might have been like if you have ever tried to speak in a language you didn't know well, or if you have tried to eat in a way that is different from how you usually eat. In my family, we eat with forks, spoons, and knives. So when I try to eat with chopsticks, it is difficult for me. If someone told me that I could never eat with forks, spoons, and knives, it would be hard. I might be able to get used to it after a while, but it would always be different from what actually felt normal to me. We call those kinds of differences *cultural* differences—and many of the things that some of the Jewish believers wanted the Gentile believers to do were things that were *culturally different* from what they were used to doing, and they were telling them so.

But not everyone agreed about this. When Paul and Barnabas heard that some people were asking Gentile believers to become Jewish, they argued about it. Paul said that God had already been working among the

Gentiles, and that many of them had believed in Jesus and began to show the fruit of the Holy Spirit in their lives, without having become Jewish. So Paul, Barnabas, and others gathered with other apostles and believers in Jerusalem to discuss the matter. We now call that the Jerusalem Council, and the big question was this: If you want to become a follower of Jesus, do you first have to become Jewish?

The decision of the council was "no." God was already showing that the Gospel of Jesus was for everyone. That idea was not a new idea: it was there in the Hebrew Bible from many, many years ago. And besides: keeping all the laws that God had given to Jewish people was always really difficult—impossible, even—and was not the way that anyone was saved. Keeping the law does not save people. People are saved by the grace of Jesus Christ, who came and kept the law perfectly, even though no one else can do that.

So it was decided that Gentile believers did not need to keep the laws that Jewish people kept. It was not a part of their culture and would be a very difficult burden for them to bear. That is not what God wants for them, since Jesus, not law-keeping, is the way to be saved.

Still, there were a few things that the people at the Jerusalem Council felt were important for Gentile believers not to do: things like eating food that had been sacrificed to false gods. These things were not simply *cultural differences*. They had to do with ways of worshiping false gods that had nothing to do with the true God. It would be best for everyone if all believers—Gentile and Jewish—avoided the things that were part of the worship of false gods.

And so Judas and Silas—some of the Jewish believers—brought this message to Gentile believers. The Gentile believers were glad to hear that they could continue to be believers in Jesus without changing all of their cultural differences—as long as they stayed away from the things that had to do with following false gods.

This story tells us once again that God's welcome is for all people, everywhere. It is not only for certain groups of people.

This story also tells us that there will be differences among different groups of believers, depending on where they live in the world and how they have grown up—what their culture is like. These differences are not wrong as long as they don't involve worshiping false gods.

Cultural differences are not wrong, as long as the most important thing is treated as most important: that Jesus is the son of the One True God, that he died, was buried, and rose again, and that he invites everyone to join his family.

Lesson 20

Romans 3:21-31; Romans 4

Salvation by Faith

What the Parent Should Know: In his epistle to the Romans, the Apostle Paul begins by asserting that no one—not Jewish people, not Gentiles—is righteous under God's law, and that, in fact, it is impossible for anyone to be so. Rather, he argues, God's law simply allows people to become conscious of their sin. As he writes: "No one will be declared righteous in God's sight by the works of the law; rather, through the law we become conscious of our sin." (3:20)

Yet all is not hopeless. Even long ago—long before Christ's incarnation— people were counted as righteous before God not so much by keeping the law, but by their faith in God. In chapter 4 of Romans, Paul uses the example of Abraham, who, we are told, "believed God, and it [his belief] was credited to him as righteousness" (v. 3; c.f. Genesis 15:6). And Abraham's righteous- ness was credited to him BEFORE he kept the law of circumcision—because he believed God, against all hope, that he would become the father of many nations, even though he was old and his wife had always been barren. Abra- ham, for Paul, becomes a model of righteousness through faith.

This doesn't mean that God's law is worthless (on the contrary, it isn't— more on that in a bit) but in addition to (and related to) his concern with establishing that the Gospel is for everyone, Paul is eager to show that right- eousness before God is emphatically NOT earned through Herculean efforts at keeping God's law, since keeping it perfectly is impossible anyway. Rather, in 3:21-31 Paul gives a concise summary of the substance of his argument in this first portion of Romans: righteousness before God now comes through faith in Jesus Christ. That is, everyone who believes that Jesus is the Son of God and that God raised Jesus from the dead (see Rom. 4:24-25) is made righteous by that faith.

> This righteousness is given through faith in Jesus Christ to all who believe. There is no difference between Jew and Gentile, for all have sinned and fall short of the glory of God, and all are justified freely by his grace through the redemption that came by Jesus Christ. (3:22-24)

And then:

> We maintain that a person is justified by faith apart from the works of the law. (3:28)

Again, in saying that people are justified by faith in Christ rather than by adherence to the law, Paul is not saying that God's law is bad, or no longer important. The law, with its many provisions for justice and mercy to the poor and vulnerable, remains significant in the life of Christian communities. Paul's point is rather that a person does not have to be circumcised and keep dietary codes in order to be righteous before God. Rather, as the example of Abraham shows, righteousness before God depends upon believing what God has promised, and, in the case of Jesus, accomplished.

Justification (being declared righteous before God) by faith, Paul suggests, is also the basis for humility. If no one, according to their deeds, can claim to be righteous before God, but instead, can only be declared righteous through their faith—their belief and trust in what Jesus has already done—there is no room for boasting (Romans 3:27), for our righteousness is ours through grace and faith. Our efforts have little to do with it, for God's grace is all.

Begin by reading aloud:

"Oh, what a good job you did cleaning the garage! I'm going to make you some hot chocolate."

"Look at how well you did on that test! I think you should get a treat."

"You practiced the violin every day this week without being told! Would you like to watch a movie tonight?"

Many times, this is how human beings judge one another. If we do good things, we believe that we are good, and that we deserve rewards. If we do bad things, we often expect punishment. To many of us, this just seems natural—the way things are.

Throughout history, people have assumed that God (or the gods, depending on their religion) was much the same way. People believed that keeping God's law perfectly was the way to be declared "righteous" (justified, all right) before God. You may remember from the stories of Jesus in *Year One* through *Year Three* that many people felt strongly that their hard work at being good and keeping the rules perfectly made them more important to God, or at least more deeply loved by God.

In his letter to the Romans, the Apostle Paul says that it is impossible for anyone to keep God's law perfectly. Instead, God's law is something like this: Imagine asking a group of people to draw as straight a line as possible without a ruler or a straight-edge, such as a hardcover book or a box. You might be able to draw a line that looks quite straight. But when you put your line next to the ruler or straight-edge, you see that it is not quite as straight as you thought. It dips and buckles here and there. That's what God's law does, Paul says: it shows us how far we are from perfect, even if, by our own lights, we seem pretty close to perfect.

But then Paul tells us that while the law is important, perfect law-keeping isn't the way that we are made righteous before God. Rather, we are made righteous by *believing* in God. If we believe, of course, we will try to do what is right in God's eyes. But believing in God comes even before following God's rules.

Paul uses the example of Abraham. Abraham lived before God had given people the whole law, or even very much of it at all. But even so, Abraham was a righteous man. He was not righteous because of his rule-following, but because he believed God, even when it was very, very difficult to believe in what God was promising him.

When God gave his law, he gave it to the people of Israel, who would later be called Jewish. Yet righteousness before God is not—and never was—just for Jewish people. It is for everyone who believes in God. And now that Jesus has come, Paul says, righteousness before God now comes through believing and trusting in Jesus Christ.

Paul says this:

"This righteousness is given through faith in Jesus Christ to all who believe. There is no difference between Jew and Gentile, for all have sinned and fall short of the glory of God, and all are justified freely by his grace through the redemption that came by Jesus Christ." (3:22-24)

And then this:

"We maintain that a person is justified by faith apart from the works of the law." (3:28)

In saying that people are justified by faith in Christ rather than by adherence to the law, Paul is not saying that God's law is bad, or no longer important. The law, which we still read in Christian churches, has so much in it about being just and kind and merciful to one another. It has many good things. What Paul is trying to say is that we do not have to keep food rules and other ritual acts in order to be righteous before God.

Instead, as Abraham's example shows us, being righteous before God means believing what God has promised. It means having faith in Jesus.

If it is true that we are justified by faith in Jesus, and not by the things we do, Paul says, then it doesn't make sense for us to brag about what we do. If we are righteous before God it is not because of what we do. It is because we have faith—we believe and trust—in what Jesus has already done for us.

Lesson 21

1 John 4:7-21

Essential Love

What the Parent Should Know: The first letter of John (traditionally thought to be the work of John the Evangelist) is, along with the books of James, Peter, and Jude, known as a "catholic" or "general" epistle, meaning that it appears not to have been written to a specific Christian community but rather to Christian communities more generally, perhaps intended as a circular letter to be read by many.

One of the preoccupations of John's first letter is to distinguish false teachers from true, and true faith from false. And love is a significant criterion for establishing the sincerity of one's faith.

John employs logical syllogisms to argue for the supremacy of love: "Let us love one another," he says, "for love comes from God."

"Everyone who loves has been born of God and knows God," and the reverse is also true: "Whoever does not love does not know God, because God is love."

The logic is simple. God is love. If you love, you know God. If you do not love, you do not know God. There can be no knowledge of God without love, because God IS love.

But what kind of love is John talking about here? He does not leave the question ambiguous, but affirms that God shows us what love is by sending Jesus into the world "that we might live through him." Love is not our feelings of affection toward God—love is God's love for us, and Jesus' willingness to come and to sacrifice himself for us. And so love, as John is using the word here, is self-giving, self-sacrifice.

And this demonstration of love in Christ's sacrifice, John says, is our model for our love of one another: "Since God so loves us, we also ought to love one another." John goes so far as to say that while none of us has ever seen God, it is this kind of love that makes God's love manifest and complete in us. How do we know what God's love is like? We look at what Jesus has done for us, yes. But we also look at the love Christians have (or ought to have) for one another.

Indeed, John reaffirms that "God is love. Whoever lives in love lives in God, and God in them." It is the dwelling spirit of God within us, he suggests, that allows us to know that God lives in us, and that we live in God. If we know this to be true, we will also be free from the fear of judgment. "Perfect loves drives out fear," John says. "There is no fear in love."

But there is another way we can be assured that God's love lives in us, and it is what John hinted at in the beginning of this passage: We know that God's self-giving love lives in us if we love our brothers and sisters. And here John's words are a challenge—not that they are difficult to comprehend, but that they are difficult to put into practice. If we claim to love God, he says, and yet hate a brother or sister, we are liars. If we love God, we are commanded also to love our brothers and sisters.

John's teaching is unambiguous. There are no loopholes or exception clauses. If we love God, we will love one another. If we do not love one another, it is evidence that we do not really love God. And we know what love is—sacrificial and self-giving—by looking at Jesus.

Begin by reading aloud:

One of my children enjoys doing science experiments. And one of the things he enjoys doing is using certain test strips to test substances for the presence of certain elements: sugar, acid, and even blood. If he puts a drop of one particular fluid onto a piece of bread and it turns black, he knows that the bread contains sugar, or a kind of sugar. If he dips a strip into lemon juice and it turns orange, he knows that the lemon juice contains acid.

Many things can be tested in this way. You have probably had a physician test your blood, or test a swab taken from your throat, to see if you were sick, or to tell what kind of sickness you might have. Women who think that they might be going to have a baby can use a test to see if their suspicions are correct.

In John's first letter, which was written almost like a newsletter, and intended to be shared among different groups of Christians, he explains several different kinds of tests that Christians can use to see if something is true or not. And one of the most important tests that he talks about has to do with love.

The test is very simple: If you love God, you will love one another. If you do not love other people, then you do not love God.

Why is this true? It is true because, as John says, "God IS love," and "love comes from God." If you SAY that you love God, but don't love other people, John says that you are not telling the truth. You are lying.

What kind of love is John talking about? He is not talking about hugs and hearts and flowers. Instead he says that Jesus shows us what God's love—TRUE love—looks like. Jesus came to earth, giving up all his privileges, and sacrificing himself to save us. That is what love is. It is self-sacrificing. It gives things up for other people.

God does not leave us on our own to try to love people in this way. Rather, he has sent his Spirit to live in us to enable us to love one another as God has already loved us.

Still, John's words are very serious. They present us with a serious test. If we say that we love God, and yet act hatefully toward other people, he says, our actions show our words to be false: we are liars.

And yet, love is also an encouraging kind of test, for if we love one another, John says, we know that God lives in us, and have nothing to fear, because, he says, "there is no fear in love" and "perfect love drives out fear."

Unit 7

The Life of the Church

Jesus' long and beautiful prayer in the Gospel according to John expresses his profound desire for unity among the believers. The model for this unity is the unity of the Godhead; Jesus prays "that all of them may be one, Father, just as you are in me and I am in you." (17:21) This unity is also described as a gift Jesus has given: "I have given them the glory that you gave me, that they may be one as we are one" (17:22) and is also meant to stand as a testimony so that "the world will know that you sent me and have loved them even as you have loved me." (17:23) The character of the shared life of Christian believers is no small matter—it is evidence of the gift of glory God shared with human beings, a testimony of the character of the love and fellowship among the members of the Godhead, and a witness to the watching world that Jesus was indeed sent by God.

This is a high calling. When faced with the divisiveness, selfishness, and bids for power that almost inevitably crop up wherever groups of people attempt to cooperate with one another, the New Testament's vision of Christian unity can seem like an impossible ideal. Even within the book of Acts, as we shall see, the seemingly idyllic early Christian community was challenged and shaken by deception and greed that ended in death. And yet though the vision of unity presented in Jesus' prayer is lofty, Christians are emphatically not left to attempt unity on their own—the Holy Spirit dwells within them, and the grace of God rests upon them.

Lesson

22

Acts 2:42-47; 4:32-37; 5:1-11; and 6:1-7

The Shared Life of Jesus' Followers

What the Parent Should Know: The book of Acts paints an astonishing picture of the common life shared by Jesus' early followers—one that continues to challenge and inspire Christian communities to this day. For not only did believers meet for worship, teaching, and prayer, but they also ate their meals together and held property and wealth in common, so that those who had much shared with those who had little.

This is described as a remarkably vibrant and joyful time, during which "everyone was filled with awe" at the signs and wonders the apostles performed; meals were eaten together "with glad and sincere hearts;" and, in spiritual fulfillment of that blessing in Genesis, "be fruitful and multiply," their number grew "daily." Luke tells us that these believers were "enjoying the favor of all the people," no doubt in part because of their open-handed generosity.

Indeed, the early believers' generosity is extraordinary—"no one claimed that any of their possessions was their own, but shared everything they had," even selling houses and land and giving the proceeds to the apostles, who distributed it to those who were in need. This is not merely extreme human generosity, Luke suggests, but is a result of "God's grace [being] so powerfully at work in them all," such that "there were no needy persons among them."

But even within Acts, we see that this early state of blissful harmony and equality is threatened by the oldest realities in human history: greed and deception. In Acts 5, Ananias and Sapphira, a married couple, sell a piece of property and give part of the proceeds to the apostles, secretly keeping some back.

When Peter accuses Ananias of this withholding, he berates him for his hypocrisy: "After it was sold, wasn't the money at your disposal?" In other words, no one asked Ananias to sell his field and give away the money. It seems that his sin is in his duplicity: wanting the appearance of gracious generosity without actually making the sacrifice. When Peter confronts him, saying that he has lied "not just to human beings but to God," Ananias falls down and dies.

Later, when Sapphira comes, Peter puts the question to her even more directly: "Is this the price you and Ananias got for the land?"

"Yes," she tells him, "that is the price."

At this Peter is furious, declaring that in this deception she has "conspire[d] to test the Spirit of the Lord." She also falls down dead, and "great fear" comes over the church and all those who hear about this unhappy event.

The Ananias and Sapphira story suggests the importance of sincerity in generosity; it is not enough to want to give the impression of open-handedness. And perhaps it highlights the necessity of divine grace in the practice of giving, as suggested in Acts 4:33. Related to this, the story may also help to clarify that true Christian giving is to be offered freely—Peter tells Ananias that his wealth is at his disposal; he is under no compulsion to give; his sin is in the deceitful way he does so.

Another story in Acts hints at further challenges. As the disciples grew in number, it became difficult for the twelve apostles to preach the Word of God and look after all of the widows in need adequately. One group felt that their widows weren't as well cared for as those in another group. At this point the apostles chose and blessed seven more individuals "known to be full of the Spirit and wisdom" to take over the responsibility of feeding those in need, offering the noteworthy suggestion that overseeing the sharing of food was regarded as serious ministry, as well.

Within the common life of believers, then, there are challenges. There are the ineradicable follies of human beings with their tendency to dissimulation. There are rivalries and grievances, and overwork. But there is also God's grace. There is also generosity and joy, and the sharing of wealth and of work and of daily bread.

Begin by reading aloud:

In the early days of the church, those who believed in Jesus didn't just "go to church" once or twice or three times a week. No, in those days, the people who made up the church lived together as a big family. They worshiped God, prayed, sang, and listened to teaching about Jesus, just as Christians do today. But for a time, they also ate all of their meals together. And they also shared everything that they had, the way families do. It would not be right to let one family member go hungry while another family member overate, would it? Or for one brother to wear three sweaters while his sister shivered and shook with cold, wearing only a t-shirt? In the same way, the early followers of Jesus lived as a family, eating together and sharing everything, in addition to worshiping God together.

Luke tells us this was a time that was very happy and full of life. More and more people wanted to join the church, which makes a lot of sense: the church was full of joyful people who took care of each other well. It was a wonderful place; a family that people wanted to join. And that is exactly what God has always wanted God's people to do: to live a life that is kind and generous; a life that welcomes other people in as if they were family.

If you are like most human beings—and most of us are very much like most of our fellow human beings in many of the important ways—sharing can feel very difficult. "MINE!" is something that children learn to say when they are quite young, and, though we might learn to be a little more polite about it as we get older, the truth is that sharing is often pretty hard, even for adults. It is easy for us to think that if we share, we will not have enough for ourselves. It is easy to think up reasons why we shouldn't have to share with other people.

That is why the generosity of Jesus' followers was so surprising; so wonderful. Luke tells us that no one thought of any of their own things as belonging to them alone, but shared everything—everything!—they had. They even sold houses and land they owned and gave the money to the apostles, who would then share that with people who were poor. How is such generosity possible? Luke tells us that God's grace was really powerful in these Christians, which means that it was as if God's own generosity was working right through these people. And because of that, there were *no* poor people among them. When things are going as God wishes them to go, and people are sharing as God shares, there is enough for everyone.

But of course, we humans do not always act as God would want us to act. Some people, Ananias and Sapphira, wanted to appear generous and still keep some of their money for themselves. So they sold some land and gave part of the money to the apostles. The only problem was that they pretended they had given everything when they really hadn't. This is a kind of lying: pretending that you are doing something really good so that others will admire you while actually cheating. Even when the Apostle Peter asked Sapphira directly whether they had given ALL the money they received for the land, she lied and said "yes." This was a serious thing: they were not honest with the family of believers, or with God.

This story may be telling us that it is important to be sincere when we are being generous. It is not enough for us to want other people to think that we are generous. We have to actually be honestly and truly generous, and for that, we need God's help.

In another story, there is more trouble: there are more and more people in the church, and it is getting harder and harder for the apostles to get all of the work done that they need to do. One group is frustrated, it seems, because the poor people among them aren't getting enough food, even though the poor people in another group are getting enough food. So the apostles choose more helpers to do the job of food sharing, which seems to be as important as the other kinds of work that the church does, like teaching and worshiping.

Just as is the case in families, in the family of believers, there are sometimes problems and hardships. Sometimes we are selfish. Sometimes we don't want to share. Sometimes some people work too hard. But, these stories tell us, God is with us, and God's grace helps us to do better: to be generous, to be joyful, to share what we have, to help one another, to eat together, and to welcome others to join us.

Lesson 23

1 Corinthians 12; and Romans 12
Sharing Different Gifts within the Community

What the Parent Should Know: The New Testament envisions the church as a single body. One person's body is made up of many diverse parts that, having vastly different functions, nonetheless work together. In a similar way, Paul describes the church as a single body—the Body of Christ—comprising many members, each of whom has particular gifts and therefore distinct contributions to make to the functioning of the body as a whole.

One of the passages that explores this idea in detail is 1 Corinthians 12. Paul begins by distinguishing between the influence of the Spirit of God and those of false gods or spirits. It is a simple distinction: If a person declares that "Jesus is Lord," he or she is speaking by the Spirit of God. If a person says something like "Jesus be cursed," he or she is definitely NOT speaking by the Spirit of God.

Paul goes on to establish the unity and diversity of the body of Christ.

There are different kind of gifts, but the same Spirit distributes them.
There are different kinds of service, but the same Lord.
There are different kinds of working,
But in all of them and in everyone it is the same God at work. (verses 4-6)

These gifts, Paul goes on to say, are given "for the common good," and include all kinds of things: wisdom, knowledge, faith, gifts of healing, miraculous powers, prophecy, discernment, and more. But even if different people have different gifts, Paul emphasizes, all "are the work of one and the same Spirit," refuting the false notion that different gifts mean that different people are being influenced by different spirits, as in some pagan philosophies.

From there Paul introduces the metaphor of the body, which powerfully evokes both the wonderful diversity and significant unity of the church—no matter our cultural background ("whether Jews or Gentiles") or our socio-economic status ("slave or free"), we were "all given the one Spirit to drink." Here Paul evokes early Christian table fellowship, which was radical in its equality and openness, as well as the Lord's Supper.

Yet, for all this unity, the body of Christ is no monoculture, but more of an ecosystem, or a complex organism comprising many different parts—"just as a body, though one, has many parts, so it is with Christ," Paul writes. And Christians are Christ's body.

Because Christians are meant to understand themselves as parts of a single body, there is no room for disunity, division, pride, isolation, envy, or disparagement of weaker or seemingly less honorable parts of the body: each has its part to play, without which wholeness is impossible. As Paul writes in the related passage, Romans 12:3-5,

> Do not think of yourself more highly than you ought, but rather think of yourself with sober judgment, in accordance with the faith God has distributed to each of you. For just as each of us has one body with many members, and these members do not all have the same function, so in Christ we, though many, form one body, and each member belongs to all the others.

And back to 1 Corinthians 12:

"The eye cannot say to the hand, 'I don't need you!' And the head cannot say to the feet, 'I don't need you.'" Paul is speaking very euphemistically, but it doesn't take much imagination to figure out that the humblest and least glamorous parts of the body are indispensable to the functioning of the whole; indeed, as Paul says, it's the most "unpresentable" parts of the body that need "special modesty." ("Do not be proud, but be willing to associate with people of low position," Paul writes in Romans 12.)

In any case, the body is a whole—if one part suffers, the whole suffers; if one part is honored, every part rejoices with it. "If it is possible, as far as it depends on you, live at peace with everyone," Paul writes in Romans 12.

Paul offers the unity of the physical human body as a metaphor for the "body of Christ" (v. 27). Not everyone will have the same gift, and that is as it should be—as indeed it must be. And if the church forms a single body, then the glue that holds it together is cooperation and love. Significantly, the chapter that follows the Corinthians passage is the famous "love chapter."

He also explains that any of these gifts, even the most spectacular and impressive of gifts, are worse than meaningless if lacking in love, because love is cooperative, inclusive, patient, and humble: the very things that make for unity within diversity.

Begin by reading aloud:

An old story I was told when I was a child went something like this:

The different parts of the body began arguing one day about which of them was the most important.

"I am the most important," said the brain. "I do all of the thinking and keep the rest of you organized."

"No, I am the most important," said the stomach. "I mash up all food and keep the rest of you all going with the energy you need."

"No, we are the most important," said the feet. "We help the rest of you move around."

And then the eyes, the ears, and many other parts of the body joined in, each arguing that their particular job was the most important thing.

The parts of the body in charge of going to the bathroom were too embarrassed to boast about their importance. After all, nobody really likes to talk about going to the bathroom. But to teach the rest of the body a lesson, they quietly decided to stop doing their job for a while.

It wasn't long before the feet began to move more slowly. The stomach began to hurt terribly. The brain felt foggy and confused. And even the eyes, the ears, and all the other parts of the body started to feel awful.

So the brain, who had started the argument in the first place, called a meeting. "We were all wrong to argue about who here is most important. We have learned that for the whole body to work well, we must all work together. Even the parts that we are embarrassed to talk about are important and necessary to us all. We couldn't do it without each other."

When he writes about the church, and the way that the people in the church should work and live together, the Apostle Paul speaks about the church in much the way this story speaks about the body. He even calls the church itself a body—the Body of Christ—which is made up of all the different people who love and follow Jesus. Each person in the Body of Christ has a different job to do, but it is a mistake to think that one job is much more important than another job.

Paul speaks about these different jobs as "gifts." You may be gifted at drawing, or making music on an instrument, or playing a sport. You can do these things well, perhaps, and not only because you have worked hard at them, but because you have a special "knack," or an inborn ability to do these things well. Similarly, Paul says that each person that is part of Christ's body has been given different gifts that he or she is meant to use for the benefit of everyone else in the body. These gifts include wisdom, knowledge, faith, understanding, hospitality, and other things.

But even if people have different gifts, Paul says, they are all meant to work together, because all of these gifts are from the same God. He writes:

> There are different kind of gifts, but the same Spirit distributes them.
> There are different kinds of service, but the same Lord.
> There are different kinds of working,
> But in all of them and in everyone it is the same God at work.

Because God is the one who gives the gifts, and because people who are part of the Body of Christ belong together, and are meant to work together, there shouldn't be any arguments about which part is more important.

Paul writes this:

> The eye cannot say to the hand, "I don't need you!" And the head cannot say to the feet, "I don't need you."

If one part of the body suffers, the whole suffers; if one part is feeling and doing well, every part other part is glad, too. "If it is possible, as far as it depends on you, live at peace with everyone," Paul writes in Romans 12.

Among the people who make up Christ's body, there shouldn't be any of the kinds of arguments that happen in the story at the beginning of this lesson.

Instead of arguing and acting competitively, members of Christ's body should try hard to work together peacefully, and with love. Paul says that all of the gifts he talks about are meaningless without love, because love is the very thing that allows different people to work together on the same task without arguing about who is the best or the most important.

1 Corinthians
Don't Be Divided: You Belong to Christ, and Christ, to God

What the Parent Should Know: Paul's letter to the church at Corinth is deeply concerned with divisions that had arisen—people had been quarrelling with one another and dividing into factions based upon who had baptized them, or who first taught them the Gospel of Jesus. "I am of Apollos," one might say; "I am of Cephas," says another. "I am of Paul," says yet another, proclaiming allegiance to these human beings much as Christians today sometimes claim denominational (or, as the case may be, non-denominational) identities and treat them as if they are of equal or greater importance to the simple identity of "Christian."

Obviously, these kinds of factions and divisions fall miserably short of the idea of the unified and harmonious life of the early church as envisioned in Acts (see Lesson 22). Nor do these divisions express the powerful image of the body of Christ as a single, unified organism, comprising different members who work together for the common good of the whole.

But Paul is concerned because these divisions reflect a serious theological misunderstanding, for to focus on the particular pastor, teacher, or minister of the Gospel is to miss the heart of the Gospel, which centers on faith in Jesus Christ. Paul emphasizes that he himself tried actively not to attract followers to himself with displays of cleverness and eloquence (1:17), so as to allow the focus to remain where it rightly belongs: on the "cross of Christ."

Indeed, Paul says, he came to the church at Corinth in fear and trembling, precisely so that their faith would not rest on human wisdom but on God. He uses an agricultural metaphor to express the reality of his ministry and that of others: He, Paul, planted the seed of faith at Corinth, and Apollos watered it, but God gave it growth, as only God can. Therefore, there is no reason to divide along the lines of who ministered to whom—if anyone's faith has blossomed, it is finally because of God.

Using another metaphor, Paul continues to establish the idea of unity in Christ: He, along with other ministers of the Gospel and other believers, are building on a foundation already laid by Jesus Christ, who is himself the foundation. Many workers may contribute, but as the hymn says, the church has but one foundation.

In any case, there is no room for boasting about "human leaders" or for declaring allegiance to one or another of them—for all these things and people already belong to each other through Christ and by virtue of being a part of the body of Christ, and belonging to God (3:21).

Paul also uses this letter to address the question of inequality of division as it relates to how the Corinthians have been practicing the Lord's Supper (ch. 11, verses 17-24). Some are going hungry, while others are overeating, and when they do this, Paul says, they are not really celebrating the Lord's Supper, because they are not acknowledging and honoring the Body of Christ. The Body of Christ, being made up of fellow believers, must not be divided, and its unity is expressed in the proper sharing of the meal. To serve an unequal or divided Lord's Supper is not to celebrate the Lord's Supper at all.

The famous "love chapter," which soon follows (ch. 13) may be seen, at least in part, as an answer and a solution to the problem of division that Paul addresses in this letter. The basis for unity is Jesus Christ, and the means of achieving it is love, by rightly recognizing that the body of Christ is one body with many members (see also Lesson 23).

Begin by reading aloud:

Imagine a group of children all playing peacefully together.

Then one of them has the idea of dividing the group according to how old everyone is. "All the eight-year-olds over here!" one child yells. "Nine-year-olds, over here!" cries another. Pretty soon the children are divided up according to their ages, and they start arguing about which group is more important. "We should be in charge because we are older!" one group says. "You have to make it easier for us because we are younger than you are!" says another.

No one is having much fun anymore, and finally, one boy calls out, exasperated, "Why does it matter who is eight or nine or ten? We are all kids!"

And of course, he is right. Their differences in age do not matter much, if at all. What matters is that they are all children, and that they are playing together. So the age-segregated groups break up, and every-one goes back to playing with everyone else.

One of the churches in the Apostle Paul's day was acting a little like those children, arguing with each other and dividing the church into groups. Those who had been baptized by Paul were in one group, those who had been baptized by a man named Apollos formed another, and yet another group was made up of those who had been baptized by someone named Cephas.

This is not at all how things are supposed to work in the church. You may remember from an earlier lesson that the early church was careful to share everything with one another, living together like a family and even eating all their meals together. The church is supposed to be the body of Christ—just like your body has different parts with different jobs to do, the church is made up of different people with different jobs to do.

But by dividing the church according to who was baptized by whom, the people at Corinth were showing that they were confused about what the Gospel was really all about. It doesn't matter who baptized you or told you about Jesus, Paul says. What matters, or rather, *who* matters, is Jesus. Paul says that in teaching the people at Corinth about Jesus, he tried not to draw attention to himself. He didn't try to be funny or clever so that people would like him and want to be his friend—he tried to get them to pay attention to Jesus and Jesus' death and resurrection. He saw himself as a messenger. What matters isn't the messenger's uniform or his hat or how he happens to knock on the door. What matters is the message. Paul didn't want people to be more interested in the messenger (him and others, like Apollos) than they were in the message.

Paul says that we should think about the people who teach about Jesus as we might think of gardeners. Some people plant the seed by telling others about Jesus. Others water the seed and take care of it by continuing to teach them about Jesus, and by sharing the good life of the church with them. But if anyone believes in Jesus and continues to grow in faith, it is because God makes them grow—just as it is only God who can make a plant grow, even if we plant the seeds and take care of them carefully.

Paul also says that the church is like a building. Many people can help build, but there is only one foundation: Jesus is the foundation.

So there is no reason, Paul says, for people to divide according to who first told them about Jesus. All of these people belong to one another through Jesus.

Also in this letter, Paul tells the people that when they celebrate the Lord's Supper, they are not doing it right because they are not sharing equally. To share the Lord's Supper is to be a part of the body of Christ. And if you are a part of the body of Christ, you must share equally, Paul says—or else you are not really celebrating Jesus' supper at all.

People have always enjoyed dividing themselves into different types of groups, and many people still do enjoy that. It can feel fun, or exciting, or important, to set yourself apart from others and form a little group. But Paul is telling us that if we are Christians, we are part of Jesus' body, which cannot be divided. He tells us that we must strive to love one another, and live at peace with one another. We do this by recognizing that, whatever our differences may be, we all belong to Jesus.

Lesson 25

What is Faith— and Why Do We Suffer?

What the Parent Should Know: In the book of Hebrews, the anonymous author gives a succinct definition of faith: the assurance of things hoped for; the conviction of things not seen.

This definition implies that faith must have an object. "Have faith that things will work out," people sometimes say, when there is, in fact, no particular reason to believe that things will, indeed, work out in the way that we might hope.

But that rather empty notion of faith has little to do with the kind of faith Christians are called to in the New Testament: faith, here, has God's promises as its object. God, who in Jesus Christ has conquered death itself, and promises to make all things new. To have faith in the New Testament sense is to continue to affirm God's goodness and God's promises, even in the absence of outward indications that would make it easier to believe that all things will truly be made new, that all things really DO work together for good (Romans 12).

Chapter 11 of Hebrews—sometimes called the "Hall of Faith" chapter— recounts biblical stories of flawed people who were, nonetheless, heroes of faith: Noah, who built an ark though he was ridiculed for doing so; Abraham, who left his home and family to go into a strange land, based only on God's promise; Moses, who rejected his princely position in Egypt to lead God's people through the wilderness, and many others.

These people of faith didn't get to see the things they hoped for, but they persevered nonetheless.

In the next chapter, the author of Hebrews urges readers to persevere through hard times, with Jesus as our example. Jesus is the supreme example of faith, enduring the suffering and humiliation of the cross "for the joy" set before him. He endured the worst, conquered death, and is now glorified with God. As other parts of Hebrews make clear, Jesus was tempted in the ways that we are, endured all that human beings endure, and yet was without sin, and continues to intercede for us.

Some of the teaching here is difficult to swallow—that suffering and struggle are ultimately for our good (the writer of Hebrews refers to suffering as God's discipline), so that we can learn holiness and obedience and reap "a harvest of righteousness and peace." (12:11) Like the great examples of faith—Noah, Abraham, Moses, and others—we cannot always see how our endurance in faith even amidst suffering will resolve into glory. But Jesus has already endured the worst, and conquered death. There is nothing so dreadful that God cannot redeem it.

Therefore, the writer urges us to believe, as we press forward in faith, that God will keep his promises; that our suffering will somehow teach us, and help our faith to grow, until such time as we receive the things we hope for— the things we don't yet see.

Begin by reading aloud:

Have you ever seen a tomato seed? If you have eaten spaghetti sauce or pizza, you may have seen one. They are very tiny, and when they are dry and ready to plant in the soil, they do not look like much at all. It is hard to believe that anything will come of putting one in the dirt and covering it up. And yet, if you have ever taken care of a garden, you know that big plants do grow from tiny seeds, if they are planted and taken care of properly.

In the book of Hebrews, the writer defines faith this way: Faith is being assured of things hoped for and yet not seen.

Christians have faith in things that we can't see—things we hope for, things we trust in God to make happen. Faith does not mean "hoping for the best." Faith is not like planting a penny in the ground and hoping that a money tree will grow from it—that's not how pennies work at all! Faith is more like planting a tiny, unlikely-looking tomato seed in the ground, taking care of it, and waiting for it to grow into a plant that bears new tomatoes.

So what is the object of Christian faith? What is the thing that Christians hope for? What is the thing that Christians are assured about, even if they can't see it?

Christians have faith in God's promises. God has already raised Jesus from the dead and has promised to conquer death itself, entirely. Even though awful things still happen, Christians have faith that all of these things will, somehow, work together for good. Christians have faith that even the worst thing—death—will one day be undone completely, because God has already begun undoing it.

The writer of the book of Hebrews—we don't know that person's name or identity—tells several stories to remind us of people who trusted in God, even when everything around them made their continued faith seem strange or even ridiculous.

Noah, for example, built an ark because God told him to do it. His neighbors laughed at him and thought he was crazy, but he did it because of his faith, because God had promised that the ark would save him and his family.

Abraham left his home and his family to move far away to a place where he knew no one, because God told him to, and promised to make Abraham's family into a great nation—even though Abraham and his wife, Sarah, were old and hadn't had any children. Abraham went because he had faith.

Moses gave up his comfortable life as something like a prince in Egypt to lead God's people through the wilderness, and he never even got to go into the Promised Land. But he did this because he had faith in God.

None of these people saw the things that they were hoping for. The way they lived surely seems strange. Why would they work hard, endure teasing and worse, and suffer discomfort and loneliness and strangeness for something they didn't even see?

They did so because of faith.

Some of the teachings in Hebrews are very hard. The writer tells us that suffering and struggles are part of what God uses in our lives so that we can learn to live well. We will not always know why we have to go through hard times, and we will not always see how those hard times will help us. What we do know is that Jesus has already endured the worst thing that anyone can endure, and conquered it: he died and conquered death, and because of this, nothing can separate us from God's love.

Living by faith means believing that God will keep his promises, even when things seem to be going badly. Living by faith means believing that the bad times will somehow teach us, and even help our faith to grow, until, finally, we receive the things we hope for—the things we don't yet see.

Lesson
26

James 2
Faith Must Express Itself
in Works, Not Just Words

What the Parent Should Know: This chapter of the epistle of James is full of themes popular with Old Testament prophets such as Amos: namely, that God demands justice and equality; that, in a reversal of the world's values, God favors people who are poor; and that faith that doesn't bear fruit in the form of good works (including relieving the suffering of people who are poor and working for justice) is dead. And these themes are interrelated.

While the New International Version (NIV) renders the first verse as saying "Brothers and sisters, believers in our glorious Lord Jesus Christ must not show favoritism," other translations, such as the New Revised Standard Version (NRSV), give a stronger sense of the absolute conflict between believing in Jesus Christ and showing favoritism and also convey an urgency and immediacy, suggesting that the letter is in response to specific acts of favoritism: "Do you with your acts of favoritism really believe in our glorious Lord Jesus Christ?"

The implication is clear: if you are showing favoritism, you are acting as if you don't believe in Jesus, because if you know anything about Jesus at all, you know that he follows an unexpected way, explicitly not showing favoritism. Or, if he does show favoritism, he does so in an upside-down way: specifically favoring those that most of the world has rejected and cast out.

James gives an example of the kind of favoritism that he is speaking against: A person comes into a gathering (presumably a gathering for worship) and, if he is dressed nicely, is given a good seat. On the other hand, a poor-looking person is made to stand, or to sit on the floor. In the Greco-Roman world, one's sitting position at the table (and remember, early church worship included a meal) indicated social rank. But Jesus' way taught a radically open and equal table fellowship—we see this in Acts, too—and so this kind of favoritism is completely out of place.

In verse 5, James hints at what some theologians have called God's "preferential option for the poor"—"Has not God chosen those who are poor in the eyes of the world to be rich in faith and to inherit the kingdom he promised those who love him?" (v. 6) Yet James' audience has, apparently, "dishonored the poor," an affront to God. "If you show favoritism," James writes in verse 9, "you sin and are convicted by the law as lawbreakers."

James continues, urging his readers to keep the law—specifically, that which urges "Love your neighbor as yourself"—and also, in light of that law, to be merciful to others. He then moves into what may be a rationale for these instructions: namely, that if you claim to have faith in Jesus, you must do good works in keeping with that faith (v. 14).

This idea—that "Faith by itself, if not accompanied by action, is dead" is related to the idea in verse 1 that if you really believe in Jesus, you will not show favoritism. One can say that one believes in Jesus, but if one then acts disdainfully toward those that Jesus loves—specifically, people who are poor—while favoring wealthy people, one's "belief" in Jesus is suspect at best. To demonstrate that words without action are empty, useless things, James uses the following example:

> Suppose a brother or a sister is without clothes and daily food. If one of you says to them, 'Go in peace; keep warm and well fed,' but does nothing about their physical needs, what good is it? In the same way, faith by itself, if it is not accompanied by action, is dead. (2:15-17)

James closes the chapter with examples from the Old Testament, Abraham and Rahab, who were considered righteous because of their good works.

Scholars and others debate whether or not James is teaching that people are saved by what they do, but for the purposes of teaching children, it is not necessary to wade into these waters. The idea that true faith will in fact bear fruit is uncontroversial. If we truly believe what we say we believe, we will live and act in accordance with that belief—and rely on God's mercy when we do not.

Begin by reading aloud:

"We love our dog so much!" the children say.

But they never remember to keep his water bowl full. When their mother asks them to take the dog for a walk, or throw the ball for him, they groan and roll their eyes.

They say they love the dog. But do their words mean anything to the dog?

Well, but dogs don't understand human speech in that way. Let's think of a different example.

"I am so sorry that you are sick, Mom! I wish I could help you feel better," a girl says to her mother.

Then her mother asks the girl to bring her a glass of cold water. But the girl is busy with something and doesn't want to get the water. "Can't my brother do it?" she asks.

She said that she was sorry her mother was sick and that she wished she could help. But did her words mean anything to her mother, when the girl wouldn't even help in a simple way?

The epistle (or letter) of James is full of teaching about words. In one chapter, James says that words are powerful, that they can be dangerous and hurtful, and that it is important to try and control the words we say.

James also tells us that words don't mean much if we don't live and behave in a way that goes along with the words we say. The children's' "love" for the dog doesn't mean much if they don't take actually help to take care of the dog.

James is concerned because the people to whom he is writing *say* they love and believe in Jesus, but aren't actually *acting* as if that is true. The way they are acting, James writes, makes it look like they don't believe in Jesus at all.

What are they doing to make their words seem false—like a lie?

They are showing favoritism. This means that they are treating some people much better than they are treating other people.

In James' world, everyone had a place in the social order. Some people—rich people, powerful and influential people—were treated as more important than other people. Other people—people who didn't have much money, people who worked as servants—were treated as less important. If you were to go into a gathering of people, you would be able to tell who the rich people were: they would have the best seats. The poor people would be standing or sitting on the floor.

But one of the things that makes Jesus' way so unexpected and upside-down is that he arranged things so that no one was to be treated as more important than anyone else. Jesus went straight for the people that no one else wanted, and invited them to share meals with him.

And we know from Acts that Jesus' followers shared everything and ate together and lived in such a way that no one was treated better because they were rich or worse because they were poor. This is how Jesus' followers are supposed to live!

But that is not what they were doing.

So James asks his readers to stop showing favoritism. And then he explains why it is so important to live and act in ways that go along with the words that they say: "Faith by itself, if not accompanied by action, is dead."

This is not so different from what James wrote earlier, about *saying* that you believe in Jesus and then showing favoritism—*doing* something that's exactly the opposite of what Jesus teaches. You can *say* all kinds of things and not mean them. It is what we *do* that shows what we really believe—what we really have faith in.

James uses this example to explain why *saying* that you believe is not enough unless you also *do* things to show that you really do believe:

> Suppose a brother or a sister is without clothes and daily food. If one of you says to them, "Go in peace; keep warm and well fed," but does nothing about their physical needs, what good is it? In the same way, faith by itself, if it is not accompanied by action, is dead. (2:15-17)

If we *say* we believe in Jesus, James says, we will *do* things that show that our belief is true and sincere. If we don't do those things, it simply reveals that we didn't truly believe in the first place.

Unit 8

After Death

Central to Christianity is the belief that Jesus, after his death and burial, rose from the dead before ascending into heaven, and that his resurrection guarantees the resurrection of the dead at the end of time. This belief of the resurrection of the dead and the life of the world to come is the foundation of Christian hope and endurance through suffering. If Christ has already conquered the worst enemy that can threaten us—death—then what else is there for us to fear? These lessons explore the centrality of the Resurrection to Christian faith, and how the belief in the death and resurrection of Jesus helps Christians to endure suffering.

<table>
<tr><td>

Lesson

27
</td><td>

Acts 9:32-43
Peter Heals Aeneas
and Raises Tabitha
</td></tr>
</table>

What the Parent Should Know: In this passage, Peter resembles Jesus to a very high degree: he heals a man who had been paralyzed and bedridden for eight years, and he raises a woman from the dead. Jesus said that his disciples (now apostles) would perform miracles and wonders in his name so that people would believe, and that is what happens here. These interrelated episodes of healing immediately precede Peter's ministry to the Gentiles.

The first part of this passage—when Peter heals a man named Aeneas from his paralysis—echoes two similar stories in the Gospels: one from John 5 and one from Mark 2. In each of those stories, Jesus heals a man who cannot walk, and tells him specifically to pick up his mat and walk.

In John's Gospel, the man Jesus heals has been unable to walk for thirty-eight years, and has been lying by the pool called Bethesda, waiting to get in first for a miraculous cure. When Jesus asks him if he wants to get well, he replies that there is no one to help him get into the pool when the water is stirred. In reply, Jesus simply tells him to get up, take his mat, and walk. This angers the religious leaders, because it is the Sabbath. In response to their judgment, Jesus declares that this healing is merely a prefiguration of greater miracles to come—such as the raising of the dead—and that it is God who is at work in him.

Mark's story is different, though it contains the similar command to "Get up, take your mat, and go." This is the man who was lowered through the roof by four friends—and Jesus, seeing their faith, said to the paralyzed man, "Son, your sins are forgiven." Teachers of the law who were present judged Jesus silently, thinking him a blasphemer, for "Who can forgive sins but God alone?" In response to their judgment, Jesus heals the man so that they may "know that the Son of Man has authority on earth to forgive sins."

Peter encounters Aeneas, telling him "Jesus Christ heals you. Get up and roll up your mat." He is clearly continuing Jesus' ministry of healing, with all the resonances of divine power, forgiveness, and wholeness that such an act suggests. It also prefigures a resurrection: that of the disciple Tabitha, also called Dorcas.

It is interesting that Dorcas' friends, distraught over her death, seek Peter—just as people distressed over death (such as Mary and Martha, the sisters of Lazarus, and the centurion) sought Jesus. People seem to understand that Jesus and his apostles have a certain authority from God over life and death, and people look to them for healing and hope in distressing situations. Peter raises Dorcas from the dead in much the same way that Jesus raises Lazarus and the daughter of the centurion: by calling her to life.

We are told, specifically, that Dorcas, a disciple of Jesus, was "always doing good and helping the poor;" and that the distraught widows, gathering around Peter to mourn, showed him "the robes and other clothing that Dorcas had made while she was still with them." These are tangible testimonies of her faithfulness that should remind us of the clothing at the resurrection of Jesus (the grave clothes folded in the tomb) and that of Lazarus (the grave clothes he still wore as he came out).

When Dorcas is raised from the dead, Luke tells us that Peter presented her to the believers, "especially the widows," just as Jesus raised people (the only son of the widow, Lazarus, the centurion's daughter) and then reunited them with their nearest and dearest, a sure indication that resurrection is in an important sense a reunion of beloved ones.

It is important to note that these resurrections, while related to Jesus' resurrection, are not the same: Jesus was raised into his resurrection body—raised "incorruptible"—while these people were raised to continue their mortal lives. They eventually died and await a final resurrection along with other departed believers.

Begin by reading aloud:

In the Gospels—the four books that tell us so much about the life and work of Jesus, and his death and resurrection—we hear many stories in which Jesus heals people, and even raises people from the dead.

And in this story from the book of Acts, a book in which Jesus' followers are continuing Jesus' work after he has returned to heaven, we can see that Jesus' followers, who are called apostles, are doing the same kind of healing, just as Jesus said that they would.

At least two times in the Gospels, Jesus heals men who cannot walk, and tells them to pick up the mats they had been lying on and to go on their way and walk! In one of these stories, Jesus heals a man who hasn't walked in thirty-eight years, and it makes people angry because Jesus heals him on the Sabbath—on a day on which no one is supposed to do any work. "Take up your mat and walk," Jesus tells him.

Jesus tells the people who are angry that they haven't seen anything yet—healing a man who cannot walk is nothing in comparison to the "greater miracles" that he will one day do: miracles like raising people from the dead.

In another one of the Gospel stories, four men lower a man who can't walk through the roof of the building where Jesus is speaking with people. Jesus tells him that his sins are forgiven. This makes people angry, because they think that only God can forgive people's sins. But Jesus IS God, of course, and that is why he can not only heal people but also forgive their sins. "Take up your mat and walk," Jesus tells the man.

By understanding the meaning of Jesus' miracles, we can also understand the meaning of Peter's miracles. Jesus' miracles showed that God was at work in and through him—and they also gave us peeks into the world that Jesus is making new: a world without injuries and sickness and death.

And so in this story, when Peter meets a man, Aeneas, who cannot walk and tells him "Take up your mat and walk," he is doing the same kind of work that Jesus does. He is doing God's work. He is helping to make the sad things in this world right.

Right after Peter heals Aeneas, some believers come to him, terribly upset. Their friend Dorcas (also called Tabitha) has died. She was a kind and generous woman who spent her time and energy taking care of people who were poor, making them clothes. "Look at the clothes she made for us," people said to Peter.

And just as Jesus raised people from the dead, Peter goes and says, "Dorcas, get up." And she gets up! Also, in the same way that Jesus returned people who had died to their loved ones, Peter quickly reunited Dorcas with the people who loved her best—the widows of whom she had taken such good care.

It is important for us to realize that these resurrections are not the same as Jesus' resurrection. When Jesus was raised from the dead, he was raised from the dead for the last time and will never die again. Dorcas and the people Jesus raised eventually died. But these miracles are still very important.

Luke tells us that the miracle of Dorcas being raised from the dead became known all over the land, and that more and more people came to believe in Jesus. That is why miracles are important. They get people's attention and surprise people. They help people to believe and to hope in the final resurrection and restoration of everything in the entire world.

Lesson

28

Romans 8:18-39

Suffering, then Glory

What the Parent Should Know: Paul ends this section of the book of Romans with a moving look at the experience and meaning of suffering in the Christian life.

As we have seen in previous lessons, the lives of many early Christians were marked by significant trials and suffering, including persecution, much as Jesus' earthly ministry culminated in suffering and death.

But in this section, Paul seems to have more in mind than the sufferings of persecution—he seems to be addressing all of the "normal" suffering that is a part of life on earth: pain and struggle and death. Paul does not limit his attention to human suffering, but insists that "the whole creation" groans in bondage to suffering, sin, and decay.

The metaphor of childbirth is integral to this passage; Paul describes creation as "groaning as in the pains of childbirth"—as do "we . . . who have the first fruits of the Spirit." It is a potent metaphor: the pain and struggle of labor gives way, in time, to a precious new life. "In this hope we were saved," Paul writes—in the hope that our present sufferings will one day give birth to a beautiful new life, and that we, along with "the creation itself," will be "liberated from [the] bondage to decay and brought into . . . freedom and glory."

Yet Paul implicitly acknowledges the difficulty of living through struggle in the meantime. "Who hopes for what they already have?" he asks. Although those who believe have the "first fruits of the Spirit," (e.g., joy, patience, faithfulness) we nonetheless, along with creation, "groan inwardly as we wait eagerly for our adoption . . . [and] the redemption of our bodies." Believers are a people living in hope between the times.

The hope that Paul insists upon here is not a false optimism, or mere "positive thinking." Rather, it is grounded in the conviction that "in all things God works for the good of those who love him;" that God held back nothing in his efforts to redeem humanity and the rest of creation, even to the point of giving his son over to death, that he might conquer death itself.

And this, the Resurrection, is the basis for hope: Jesus who died and was raised to life sits at the right hand of God interceding for us (v. 34). In light of the Resurrection, what can separate us from God's love? Death has been conquered, so what can "trouble or hardship or persecution or famine or nakedness or danger or sword" do to us? Nothing "in all creation" can separate us from God's love in Jesus Christ.

This does not mean that our "present sufferings" (v. 18) are meaningless, or not worth mentioning because God will make everything all right in the end. Knowing that "God works all things together for good" doesn't mean that we will understand the reason for terrible suffering. After all, hope would not be hope if we already knew exactly how our suffering was going to be transformed into something glorious and beautiful.

What we do know is this: In the Incarnation, God suffered with and for us to conquer death and to give us—and this old earth—rebirth and redemption, and not even death itself can separate us from that tremendous, transformative love that is in Christ Jesus.

Begin by reading aloud:

Not long ago, one of my children had to have a cavity filled at the dentist.

Most of the time, the dentist can give you certain medicines that make it so that you don't feel anything at all. But this time, the medicine wasn't working very well, so my son felt some pain. He cried and clenched his fists, being very brave. Finally, it was all over, and his cavity was filled.

"I really suffered, Mom," he told me. "That was terrible."

We talked about how awful it is to feel scared and to be in pain. And then we talked about how getting cavities filled is a good thing. The dentist gets the rottenness and decay that is in your tooth out, cleans it, and fills the tooth with something that keeps the tooth strong and healthy.

So there is a reason for the pain and discomfort we might experience at the dentist. It is to take what is unhealthy and make it whole and healthy again.

Not all painful or uncomfortable or sad things are like this. Many times, people and animals suffer and there seems to be no good reason for it at all. Maybe you have seen a bird with a broken wing or a hurt leg. Maybe a pet that you loved has died. You may even have lost a person that you knew.

In his letter to the believers at Corinth, the Apostle Paul writes about suffering. As you have already learned, the lives of the early Christians were full of trials and suffering. And as you may already know just from being alive, everyone experiences pain and suffering sometime in their life. Paul says that God's whole creation—the whole world and everything in it—groans and suffers.

But Paul also says that this groaning and pain is like the pain of childbirth. When a mother has a baby, it usually hurts for a while. When it is all over, though, there is a baby: a new life! When my son was at the dentist, it hurt for a while, too, but when it was all over, his tooth was as good as new. Paul is saying that the pain and struggle that we all go through now is going to end up very good, somehow. Paul writes that "the creation itself" will be "liberated from [the] bondage to decay and brought into . . . freedom and glory."

It is a difficult thing to believe: suffering and pain and death will be transformed into something good? Paul knows that. That is why he says Christians live in hope—and hope is not something you have if you already can see for yourself that everything has already turned out all right. Hope lives where you are still in pain, still in the dentist's chair, waiting and hoping for your tooth to be made better and whole once again.

But why should Christians have hope? Not because bad things aren't really all that bad. No, Christians can have hope, Paul writes, because God is always, always with us, no matter what. God held nothing back when he set to work to repair and redeem this world—to make it all new and beautiful.

As you have heard from other lessons, it is Jesus' death and resurrection that shows us this truth most clearly. If God is willing to become a man, to die, and then to defeat the enemy of death by rising again, what is there that God cannot do? What is there that can separate us from God's love?

The answer is that nothing can separate us from God's love. There is no suffering or hurt or loss that God cannot heal and make new. In becoming a person, God suffered with us, and for us, so that he could destroy death and heal this whole world from pain and decay, and make it whole again—better than new—and beautiful.

Lesson 29

1 Thessalonians
Living Between the Times; Grieving, but with Hope

What the Parent Should Know: Paul's first letter to the church of the Thessalonians is a letter of encouragement to a relatively young Christian community that already seems to have faced substantial challenges, including persecution, and yet also seems to be flourishing in ways that can only suggest the Holy Spirit is at work in them. They are growing in faith and their love toward one another is increasing. In this letter, Paul wants to encourage them to continue persevering in hope and in joy, urging them to live well as they wait for Jesus' return. It is, Paul suggests, the Word of the Lord and the living witness of the Holy Spirit that makes this possible.

One of the strongest themes in the letter is the love and affection—indeed, the familial bonds—that shared faith in Christ fosters. Repeatedly, Paul emphasizes that he and the others (including Silvanus and Timothy, as named in 1:1) pray for the believers at Thessalonica and that they love them very much, with a familial love (Paul speaks of himself as both mother and father to the young church). Related to this, Paul repeatedly expresses the hope that they may grow in love for one another, for that love would seem to be the basis of the kind of life they are called to as they wait for Jesus' return: a life that involves loving others well, minding one's own business, and working diligently so as to be able to provide for oneself (and, as Paul emphasizes elsewhere, so as to be able to share with others).

Another important theme in the letter is the reality of persecution, which the Gospels, Acts, and Paul all treat as an expected part of the Christian life: "Indeed, you yourselves know that this is what we are destined for," Paul writes in 3:3. He speaks also of the risk that he and the others took even in preaching to the Thessalonian church (2:2). Paul notes that he was especially worried that they might have been tempted and fallen away from the faith when the trials came their way, but he was so encouraged and joyful to learn that they have, in fact, continued in their faith. During their own distresses and persecutions, knowing that the church at Thessalonica is remaining strong is a great encouragement. Bad times will come, and no one should be surprised at that (5:4), but the believers are to remain strong in hope and in a life lived in love.

These themes are significant, but the center of Paul's encouragement and exhortation is Christ's resurrection, which is the basis for the faith, hope, and love that Paul urges. Even severe persecution that ends in death does not spell the death of hope because just as Jesus died and rose again, so also, through Jesus, God will raise those who have died, and gather even those who are alive to himself. "Encourage one another with these words," Paul says. Indeed, as elsewhere (see Lesson 30) in the New Testament, the resurrection from the dead and the promise of resurrection bodies that will no longer be subject to death and decay is the center of the Christian hope; the anchor of the soul.

To press on in love and hope and faith when everything around you is difficult and discouraging—when people are, in fact, attacking you for your faith—requires more than just a firm resolve to live in a certain way. It requires the comfort and aid of the Holy Spirit, the help of "the God of peace," and the grace of the Lord Jesus Christ, all of which Paul prays for his dear church.

Begin by Reading Aloud:

You may remember from other lessons that Christians were to expect to be persecuted; that is, to be taunted or harmed for believing in Jesus. Jesus himself told his followers to expect that this would happen.

It is strange to think that anyone would suffer what early Christians suffered if they didn't really believe that Jesus was God's son, and that

Jesus had risen from the dead. But more and more people came to believe in Jesus, and, when they were persecuted, to continue believing.

Today, if you live in North America or in Europe or in parts of Africa and South Asia, you see churches and crosses everywhere: people who believe in Jesus are everywhere, and even where many people don't actually believe in Jesus, they don't much mind if other people do. They are used to having Christians around. But in these early days of the church, believing in Jesus was seen as something dangerous. It was new and threatening. People didn't like it.

And yet, people kept on believing and following the way of Jesus. As the Apostle Paul (who, you may remember, started out as a persecutor of the church himself) traveled and taught, more and more people began to believe and form little groups of believers—what we would call "churches." Even after he left, Paul wanted to keep teaching them. He cared for them very much—as much as a mother or a father cares about his or her children. He tried to visit when he could, though he couldn't always do that. So he wrote letters, and this is one of them.

The church of the Thessalonians seems to be a new church, a "young" church—it hasn't been long since the believers there first believed in Jesus. But they are doing very well. They are already facing the persecution that Christians can expect to face, yet they are still believing in Jesus, still acting in loving and kind ways to one another, still growing in their faith, as Paul says, meaning that they are believing more and more firmly in Jesus and loving and living better and better. They are even joyful, Paul says.

To be joyful even when people are harming you; to continue believing in Jesus even when it would be easier for you not to do that—these things are not exactly natural. They show us that the church at Thessalonica really believed, but they also show us something else: that the Holy Spirit of God was with this group of people, making them strong.

Paul has a lot of good things to say to this young church. They may be young, but they are doing very well. They are joyful even when things are hard. They care for and love one another. So Paul mainly wants to encourage them to keep going as they are going, even when bad times come.

What makes it possible for people to keep going? What makes it possible for people to keep loving one another and believing in God even when everything around them is bad, or even horrible, and when people they love die?

What makes it possible is Jesus' resurrection. That Jesus died and then rose from the dead gives us reason to hope. Jesus died and rose again, and so also, through Jesus, God will raise up those who have died. Jesus has conquered and taken care of the worst thing that can happen—death, promising that those who die will be raised from the dead in new bodies that can never die. This is what makes Christians hopeful even when things around them are bad.

But to hope in the Resurrection, to have faith in God, and to love one another in this world where so many bad things happen is not always easy. That is why Paul prays for the churches, and asks God to help them. If we believe in Jesus, we can have faith that God will help us to love one another and live well and to keep hoping for God to make everything right even when things look bad.

Lesson

30

1 Corinthians 15
The Importance of the Resurrection

What the Parent Should Know: This passage establishes unequivocally that the center of the Christian faith is the death, burial, and resurrection of Jesus: This is the truth that Paul has taught "as of first importance," and he spends the chapter arguing for the central importance of the Resurrection.

It's important to note that when Paul talks about resurrection in this chapter, he is speaking both of Jesus' resurrection (which has already happened) and of the (future) resurrection of those who believe in Jesus.

This teaching was in response to specific concerns: some people had, apparently, been saying that there is no resurrection; indeed, even in the Gospels we know that there were pockets of resurrection-deniers (such as the Sadducees) even while other traditions believed in a resurrection of the dead.

Paul begins by affirming the singular significance of the Resurrection, and also (verses 4-8) by establishing the fact that there were many eyewitnesses to the Resurrection: "He appeared to Cephas, and then to the Twelve. After that, he appeared to more than five hundred of the brothers and sisters at the same time," most of whom are still alive. He has even appeared to Paul, albeit, Paul acknowledges, in a strange way.

Then Paul argues that the Christian faith would be nonsensical without resurrection. To deny the resurrection of dead people is to deny the resurrection of Christ. And if Christ has not been resurrected, then everything that he and others have believed and preached and taught about (and even died for) is useless. And that is serious—it constitutes bearing false witness against God, Paul argues—"for we have testified about God that he raised Christ from the dead." Paul affirms this line of argumentation once again, effectively establishing that the resurrection—first of Christ, then of those who believe in Christ—is the sine qua non of Christian faith.

Affirming once again that "Christ has indeed been raised from the dead," Paul goes on to explain what that means for all of us: namely, that the inescapable end of humankind—death—will be finally conquered by Jesus as "the last enemy to be destroyed." In dying and being raised from the dead, Jesus is a "first fruits" of those who have already died: he shows us what resurrection looks like.

What will resurrection bodies look like? Paul's answers are not overly specific, but it is clear that whereas the bodies we have now are subject to illness and injury and death, our bodies then will be "raised imperishable." Paul isn't saying that the bodies we have now are bad (he says they have a splendor of a certain kind) only that the splendor of resurrection bodies will be a different splendor.

Whatever those resurrection bodies will be like, they will be physical bodies—Paul is not envisioning some kind of spiritual resurrection where disembodied souls float about together in some alternate universe. When he says in verse 50 that "flesh and blood cannot inherit the kingdom of God," he is not disparaging physical bodies, but rather, saying that we must be transformed into the image of Christ in his resurrection body—turned from the desires and drives of a merely this-worldly existence and toward resurrection life. Even those who have not yet died when Christ returns are going to be changed somehow—are going to be clothed with the imperishable, with immortality.

And what does this mean for us right now? Certainly, it means that we have hope for the future: that death is not the end. But resurrection is not just a future hope. It is also, in Christ, an accomplished fact, a reality. He has already conquered death. This, Paul seems to be arguing, should give us strength and fortitude. "Stand firm," he writes. "Your labor in the Lord is not in vain."

The point is emphatically not that we are going to die and then be raised, so we may as well live as we please. Rather, the central truth of the Christian faith means that God is making everything new, and that we who believe get *to participate in that process of making all things new. What we do in the Lord—even if we die doing it!—is not in vain.*

Begin by Reading Aloud:

There is a book I read to my children about birds. Again and again, it asks the question, "What makes a bird a bird?"

You may say, "A bird is a bird if it flies!"

But of course, lots of creatures that aren't birds can fly: mosquitoes, butterflies, and bats. And some creatures that are birds can't fly—ostriches, for example.

So you may say "A bird is a bird if it lays eggs!"

But of course, other animals lay eggs—lizards and fish and spiders.

Finally, the book tells us what makes a bird a bird, and you have probably already guessed: feathers! Without having (or, in the case of plucked birds, without having had) feathers, a bird is not a bird.

In this chapter of his letter to the church at Corinth, the Apostle Paul is not teaching people about birds, of course, but he is trying to explain something that is as important to the Christian faith as feathers are to birds: without this thing, he is saying, the Christian faith is really not the Christian faith.

What is this thing that is to Christian faith as feathers are to birds? It is resurrection, which to Christians means two things.

First, resurrection, for Christians, means the rising of Jesus from the dead, which has already happened.

Second, for Christians, resurrection means the future rising of those who have died, which Christians believe will happen because it has already happened to Jesus.

Some people had begun teaching that there would be no resurrection at all, and Paul wants to show that this teaching is wrong—and that without the resurrection, there really is no Christian faith.

Paul begins by saying that many, many eyewitnesses saw the Resurrection. Jesus appeared alive after his death and burial to many people, including a group of more than five hundred men and women, most of whom were still alive when Paul wrote this letter. It is as if Paul is suggesting that his readers go ahead and ask around—there were many people who saw Jesus and know the Resurrection to be a true event.

Then Paul argues that, without resurrection, the Christian faith makes no sense. If we say that it is impossible for people who die to someday be raised from the dead, it is like saying that Jesus could not have been raised from the dead. And if Jesus was not raised from the dead, then everything that Paul and so many others have been living for and preaching and going to prison for and even dying for means nothing at all. A bird is not a bird without feathers. Christianity is not Christianity without the Resurrection. It is that important.

So what does that mean for us?

It means that the terrible thing that ends all of our lives, and separates us from the people we love, will one day be over—"swallowed up." Jesus has been raised from the dead, and this fact shows us a picture of what resurrection will be like.

But what will our resurrection bodies really be like? Paul doesn't tell us, exactly, except to say that while our bodies now can get sick and hurt and damaged and eventually die, our bodies then won't do any of those things—they will be "raised imperishable."

We do know, however, that we can expect to have real, physical bodies. Sometimes people imagine that "life after death" means that our soul or our mind or whatever it is that makes us ourselves but that can't be seen or touched will be floating invisibly around "somewhere." That is not what Paul or Jesus has in mind at all. We can expect bodies something like the ones we have now, but ones that won't ever wear out or stop working.

What does this mean for us right now? For one thing, it means that we have hope for the future, even when sickness and death come into our lives. But even more than that, Paul wants us to know that resurrection is not just a future hope. It is something that has happened to Jesus already. And knowing that can help us to be strong and brave. Jesus has already conquered death.

"Stand firm," Paul tells us. "The things you do for God are not for nothing."

Not only is God making everything new, but God also lets us help. When we do what Jesus did—feed hungry people, bring thirsty people water, comfort people who are suffering—we are helping the world to look a little bit more like the resurrection world that Christians hope for.

Without the Resurrection, Christianity is not Christianity. We live with hope, because of what Jesus has already done. And we live like people who know that, even now, things are being made new.

Unit 9

Last Things

The book of Revelation confounds many people, even those who have been raised in the Christian faith. Some of its apocalyptic imagery is perplexing and bizarre, even frightening, particularly when it is envisioned—as it has been by Hollywood—as something along the lines of science fiction.

Looked at a bit differently, the book of Revelation offers an important vision of the end of time: of the risen and exalted Christ in his glory, of the Garden of Eden transported into the City of God that fills the whole Earth, and of the intimate relationship between God and people when, at last, death has been conquered once and for all and every tear has been wiped away.

Lesson **31**	**Revelation 1, especially verses 12-20** **Christ, the Mighty** **Conquering One**

What the Parent Should Know: Often enough, we have a mental picture of Jesus as entirely meek and mild, even a bit puny. While we seem to have little trouble envisioning the baby in the manger, or the crucified Christ, imagining the risen Christ is somewhat more difficult. What does it mean that Jesus has died, but has been raised, incorruptible, so that he will never die, and is, in fact, alive even now?

The book of Revelation, though written in highly figural language, is, in fact, the revelation of Jesus Christ. This is one reason why the book is not called RevelationS, plural, but rather the revelation, singular, of the one Lord Jesus Christ, given to the churches through John, who, as a result of persecution, is in exile on the island of Patmos. Jesus appears to him and charges him with writing his vision and sharing it with the "seven churches," which are representative of ALL the churches (seven being a biblical number expressing completeness or wholeness).

John's vision begins with hearing, from behind him, a loud voice like a trumpet. Turning to look, he sees a truly remarkable sight:

> [W]hen I turned I saw seven golden lampstands, and among the lampstands was someone like a son of man, dressed in a robe reaching down to his feet and with a golden sash around his chest. The hair on his head was white like wool, as white as snow, and his eyes were like blazing fire. His feet were like bronze glowing in a furnace, and his voice was like the sound of rushing waters. In his right hand he held seven stars, and coming out of his mouth was a sharp, double-edged sword. His face was like the sun shining in all its brilliance. (verses 13-16)

This image is kingly and fierce: eyes of fire; a mouth from which emerges a sharp sword (presumably, because it is a mouth that cannot but divide truth from lies—a sharp sword being a metaphor for truth-telling). In this vision, Christ looks a lot like the God of the Old Testament: strong and victorious. This is the vision that sets up everything else in the book of Revelation, as everything in heaven and earth is put into order by this mighty, triumphant King.

John is, quite understandably, afraid at this vision ("I fell at his feet as though dead," he writes). Yet as he does in the Gospels, when appearing to his disciples after the Resurrection, Jesus urges John not to fear. Jesus' presence is, in fact, the basis for leaving aside fearfulness entirely:

> "Do not be afraid," Jesus says. "I am the First and the Last. I am the Living One; I was dead, and now look, I am alive for ever and ever! And I hold the keys of death and Hades." (verses 17-18)

Jesus is completely triumphant, and he is standing there, among the lampstands, which are the churches. What does the church have to fear, if

THIS is the one who walks among them, utterly powerful and mighty, yet gentle and loving?

Again, we often forget that Jesus is mighty in his resurrection. He is not an endlessly patient, avuncular fellow. Here the revelation of the risen Lord is that of a powerful, triumphant warrior king who has conquered the last, worst enemy—death—and who now dwells among the churches. What can anyone do to the one to whom Jesus stands with? He holds the keys to death and hell!

So, in the face of the difficulties and persecutions to come, the church need not fear. This warrior king triumphant stands among us, and he is for us.

Begin by Reading Aloud:

There are two ways that people have of speaking about Jesus that make it difficult to understand who Jesus really is: speaking of Jesus in the past tense, as if he were no longer alive, and speaking of Jesus and what Jesus would do as if Jesus is just a generally nice man who mostly wants people to have good manners, but who is not particularly strong or bold.

At Christmastime we think about Jesus as a baby in a manger. At Easter we think about Jesus on the cross, and then in the garden, greeting his friends. At Pentecost we think of him disappearing into the clouds and going up into heaven. But then what? What happens next?

In this part of the Bible, the Apostle John has a vision of Jesus as he is in heaven. And he is not a baby in a manger. He is not a generally nice man who mostly wants people to have good manners. And he is definitely not a person to be spoken of in the past tense. The Jesus that John sees in a vision and then writes about is a powerful, even frightening figure.

John's vision begins with hearing, from behind him, a loud voice like a trumpet. Turning to look, he sees Jesus—who appears truly remarkable:

> [W]hen I turned I saw seven golden lampstands, and among the lampstands was someone like a son of man, dressed in a robe reaching down to his feet and with a golden sash around his chest. The hair on his head was white like wool, as white as snow, and his eyes were like blazing fire. His feet were like bronze glowing in a furnace, and his voice was like the sound of rushing waters. In his right hand he held seven stars, and coming out of his mouth was a sharp, double-edged sword. His face was like the sun shining in all its brilliance. (verses 13-16)

This word-picture paints Jesus as kingly and fierce—something like a very strong superhero. He has fiery eyes, a mouth that is like a sharp sword (which probably means it is a mouth that can only speak the truth), and a face as bright as the sun. He glows, and he stands among the lampstands and stars, which John tells us represent the churches and the angels that watch over the churches. This is Jesus after his resurrection, in a body that will never die, powerful and strong, ready to put everything in heaven and on earth into order.

John tells us he was pretty afraid of Jesus at this point—"I fell at his feet as though dead," John writes—and that makes sense: Jesus looks powerful and a bit scary. But just as he did when he appeared to his friends and disciples after he rose from the dead, Jesus tells John not to be afraid. Jesus is powerful beyond measure, strong beyond imagining, but he is gentle. He brings peace. And his presence is the very thing that can allow us to leave aside our fears, because Jesus has already taken care of the worst thing that there is in this world: death.

"Do not be afraid," Jesus says to John. "I am the First and the Last.
I am the Living One; I was dead, and now look, I am alive for ever and ever! And I hold the keys of death and Hades." (verses 17-18)

Jesus is completely triumphant, and he is standing there, among the lampstands, which are the churches. What does the church—what do Christians—have to fear, if THIS JESUS is the one who walks among them (and among us), utterly powerful and mighty, yet gentle and loving?

We should not forget that Jesus is mighty in his resurrection. He appears to John, and, through John's writings, to us, as a powerful, triumphant warrior king who has conquered the last, worst enemy—death—and who now dwells among the churches; among us. What can anyone do to us if Jesus stands with us? He holds the keys to death and hell!

So, in the face of the difficulties, we do not need to be afraid. Jesus, a warrior king triumphant, stands among us, and he is for us.

Revelation 21

God Makes All Things New

What the Parent Should Know: Thanks to its apocalyptic character, the book of Revelation has often been sorely misunderstood: envisioned as something akin to a science fiction or fantasy adventure. Consequently, many people find the book perplexing and even frightening, which many parts of it may be, if you press the details too firmly. But this is deeply unfortunate, because the concluding vision of Revelation is as glorious—and as comforting—as anything else in all of scripture, for it is here that we see the ultimate reality upon which Christian hope depends: the final defeat of death, once and for all; the elimination of suffering and mourning and pain; and, best of all, the intimate union of God with God's people.

The natural background to the closing passages of Revelation, which are the closing passages of the Bible, are the opening passages of the Bible. Even more, these closing passages are the consummation of the overarching story of Scripture. In Genesis, God creates the world out of love, and creates human beings to live in fellowship with him. That fellowship is ruptured, of course, in the story of the expulsion from Eden, and this rupture is repeated again and again. God wants to dwell with his people and to recapture the lost fellowship of Eden, but it is not to be—human frailty gets in the way again and again. God cannot dwell in temples made of human hands. And when God dwells among humans in the form of Christ, he, too, is rejected and killed, though of course he conquers death, securing the hope that death may finally be conquered.

And it is here, in Revelation 21, that we see the realization of these long-expected hopes—a "new heaven and a new earth," the Holy City, "the new Jerusalem;" fulfilling the role they were always meant to have: to be the dwelling place for human beings and for their God. "Look! God's dwelling place is now among people, and he will dwell with them. They will be his people, and God himself will be with them and be their God." (verses 2-3) As the scholar Luke Timothy Johnson notes, in Jewish tradition, no one could look at God, or even speak God's name. (This is still true of Orthodox Jews; you will hear them speak of "hashem"—"the name"—but they do not speak or write the name of God.) So the vision in Revelation is almost scandalous in its intimacy: here is God, dwelling among his people.

More than that, Revelation 21 offers the suggestion that God himself will care tenderly for his people, even wiping tears from their eyes. Perhaps this is reminiscent of the fact that, after his resurrection, Jesus bore the wounds of his crucifixion. Similarly, in the New Earth, people's eyes may still shed tears over the things they have suffered—but God himself will wipe those tears away. Moreover, "there will be no more death or mourning or crying or pain." This is, of course, a reversal of the Eden story, when death and mourning and crying and pain entered into the world. This order, this "old order of things," will have passed away (v. 4), and the one who sits on the throne—that is, Christ—is making all things new, ready to give those who are thirsty drinks from the spring of the water of life. Overall, it is a picture of the Garden of Eden restored.

But the description of the Holy City, Jerusalem, is also reminiscent of how the temple in the Old Testament is described—specifically, its cube-like measurements reveal it to be architecturally similar in its proportions to the Holy of Holies—except now, the Holy of Holies fills the whole city. That is why there is no temple—no set-apart place of holiness, because the Lord God IS the temple. There is no place in the entire city that is not holy. Nor is there need for sun or moon, for God's radiance provides all the light that is needed. This is the New Creation, the life that God has always desired to share with God's people: no more suffering, no more death, no more darkness or night—and no more separation between God and God's people. It is a beautiful vision: the city becomes the Garden of Eden and the Holy of Holies, and rather than having God's face and God's name hidden from them, God's people will live close to God, who will tenderly care for them as God has always longed to do.

Begin by reading aloud:

From the very beginning of the Bible—in the book of Genesis—God has always wanted to be near to human beings. He made the world and everything in it, including people, and wanted to live alongside them.

But again and again, in the stories of the Bible, people have misunderstood God. They have been foolish and selfish. They have not listened to God. They have not tried to do what God asked them to do.

God has never given up. God sent prophets to tell his people that they were being unfair to people who are poor; that they were being selfish and greedy; that pleasing God didn't mean keeping all the rules perfectly, but meant loving God, being humble, and treating others justly.

And this made many of God's people very angry with the prophets. They didn't want to hear that there was anything wrong with how they were living at all. Many times, people were so angry with the prophets that they had them killed.

So God sent his son, Jesus, to show people who God really is. And this was a remarkable thing: God became a human being, Jesus, who lived among human beings and went through all the things human beings go through: being tired, hungry, worn out, and in pain.

And, like the prophets before him, Jesus was even put to death for saying and doing the things he did. But he also rose from the dead, promising that the old, worst enemy—death—would one day be destroyed.

In the final chapters of the Bible, John's vision shows us God's plan for the conclusion of the story. We can see clearly what it is that Christians hope for. We hope for the final defeat of death. We hope for the ending of pain and suffering and tears. We hope to be with God forever and ever.

This is how God always wanted it to be. And this is how it will be one day. The language that John uses in the book of Revelation is like poetry. It doesn't tell us exactly how everything will be, but it gives us a good idea. God will be with us. God will wipe away our tears. And in this new city that God will build for us, to live among us, there will be no more death, no more crying, no more pain—again, just the way God always wanted it to be.

Lesson 33

Revelation 22

Come, Lord Jesus

What the Parent Should Know: At the beginning of Acts, when Jesus ascends to heaven, his disciples stand staring into the sky. "Why do you stand staring at the sky?" the angel asks them. He explains that Jesus will return, just as he has left. And in the meantime, the disciples—then apostles—are charged with continuing Jesus' work through the constant help and presence of the Holy Spirit. In this, the final chapter of the New Testament—and therefore of the Christian Scriptures—the reader is urged not to stand staring at the sky, as it were, but to live in light of Jesus' declaration, "Look, I am coming soon!"

This promise, "I am coming soon," is repeated three times in the chapter. The first time, it is followed by an invitation to obedience—to "keep the words of the prophecy written in this scroll." The second time Jesus says that he is coming soon, he promises that his reward will come with him, and that he will "give to each person according to what they have done." The final time, the promise of Jesus' "coming soon" follows a stern warning not to add to or take away from the words of the prophecy of this book, and John, the author, adds his affirmation: "Amen. Come, Lord Jesus," and a blessing of grace upon God's people—upon the people who are, like him, waiting for Jesus' return, and hoping that it will be soon.

The repetition of the concept that Jesus is coming soon underlines its importance. Christians do not simply worship a wise man that was crucified, who died, and was buried—and remained buried. Christians worship and follow a living Jesus, a Jesus who promised that he would be coming soon. It goes without saying that the years have indeed been very long since this vision of John's; since John recorded Jesus' promise that he would be coming soon and his own yearning prayer, "Come, Lord Jesus." Still, Christians do wait for Jesus' return, trying to live in light of this expectation, continuing in the way that the apostles did: with the help of the Holy Spirit, extending the testimony and deeds of Jesus throughout the world.

It is not hard to see how the final chapter of the Bible recalls the Garden of Eden: The river of the water of life flows from the throne of God, through the middle of the city, and along the banks of the river grows the tree of life, which yields a crop of fruit every month; its leaves, we are told, "are for the healing of the nations." The vision is like that of Psalm 1, where the righteous person, who loves the Word of God, is like a fruitful tree. But it is also something of a reversal: No longer do angels block access to the tree of life, as in Genesis 3; rather, its leaves are for the healing of all the many wounds humankind has suffered, and inflicted, in the meantime. It is a beautiful and remarkable vision: a peaceable city where tears are wiped away, wounds are healed, and nothing gets in the way of God's presence among God's people.

While this chapter has stern warnings for those who refuse to heed its words, it also explicitly echoes the hospitable welcome of Isaiah 55. "Let the one who is thirsty come; and let the one who wishes take the free gift of the water of life," John writes in 22:17. This is not a picture of a God who is eager to cast people out. On the contrary, this is a picture of a God who delights to welcome people in.

This final chapter does not answer every question people may have about the life of the world to come. But it does show us a restored earth, a Garden of Eden made new, and a hospitable God who wants to welcome us in. And it urges us to regard this city—and Jesus' return—with hopeful expectation.

The one who says "I am coming soon" also bids weary, thirsty people to come to this city of healing; this city through which runs the water of life.

And so Christians do not live staring absently at the sky. Christians live in expectation of this future reality, of Jesus' imminent return, and of God's profoundly hospitable welcome.

This picture of peaceful, healing, beautiful welcome and intimate relationship with God is the concluding vision of the New Testament, and the substance of Christian hope.

Begin by reading aloud:

I never like to say goodbye to people. Even when I know that it is going to be a very long time before I see them again, I always want to say "I'll see you later!" instead of "goodbye." Goodbye feels far too final and sad, as if you might not ever see the person again.

At the beginning of this book, Jesus went up into heaven, and his friends were gathered around staring at the spot in the sky where he had disappeared from their sight. Can you imagine how they must have felt?

Even though Jesus had explained things to them, they didn't quite understand. They were staring into the sky, but Jesus had given them important work to do—to continue the work that Jesus had begun: teaching and preaching and healing and feeding—until Jesus returns.

In this final chapter of the Bible, the author, John, reminds us three times that Jesus is returning soon. And when he returns, all of that work—the teaching and preaching and healing and feeding—will come to an end, because God will have healed every wound, and God will feed everyone, and no one will any longer need to be taught about God because they will live with God.

If Jesus says in this book—this very old book!—that he is coming soon, why hasn't all of this happened yet? Why are Christians still waiting for Jesus to come?

No one can answer that question. We do know that time is nothing at all to God, so that for God, a thousand years is like a day, and a day is like a thousand years. So perhaps the word "soon" doesn't mean the same thing to God as it does to us.

Still, Christians *do* wait for Jesus to return. And while we wait, we try to live the way the apostles did: with the help of the Holy Spirit, we try to live in the world as Jesus did.

The final chapter of the Bible, unlike the final chapter of most other books, doesn't tell us how it all ended. It tells us how it is *going* to end. And the way John describes it, it sounds very much like the way it began in the Garden of Eden: God is there, with his people, there is abundant fruit on the tree of life, and there is a river flowing through the city to quench the thirst of anyone who wishes to come.

"Let the one who is thirsty come; and let the one who wishes take the free gift of the water of life," John writes in 22:17. This is not a God who is eager to cast people out. No, this is a God who loves to welcome people.

This final chapter does not answer every question we may have about the life of the world to come. But it does show us a restored earth, a Garden of Eden made new, and a hospitable God who wants to welcome us home.

And it also shows us that we should not think about the story of Jesus as being a story that is over and done, and in the past. We should not think about Jesus as someone to whom we have all said "goodbye."

No, we should not think of this as something that is over and done, because Jesus says to us, "I am coming soon." And he invites us—whoever we are—to come to him.

Unit 10

These Three Remain: Faith, Hope, and Love

In the famous "love chapter" of 1 Corinthians 13, the Apostle Paul, in establishing the absolutely essential character of love, names three things that remain after other gifts (including prophecies, tongues, and knowledge) pass away. We may know in part, and prophesy in part, "but when completeness comes, what is in part disappears." For now, in our Christian lives, we know only in part; we "see only a reflection as in a mirror," though someday we will "see face to face" and understand fully "even as [we] are fully known." But for now and for always, faith, hope, and love remain, superseding knowledge and tongues and prophecy in their eternal significance. The "faith, hope, and love" formula is frequently and justifiably invoked as expressing the essential features of Christian discipleship. And yet the meaning of these terms is not always clear. This unit explores each of these qualities with the aim of clarifying what the Christian tradition has taken them to mean.

What the Parent Should Know: Scholars describe the New Testament's word for faith—forms of which are often translated as "belief"—as a hybrid of noun and verb, both an idea and an action. In popular discourse, people sometimes speak of faith as if it is purely a state of mind, and while Christians of different traditions have debated the meaning of faith, it seems clear from the New Testament that faith indeed involves both idea and action.

New Testament scholar N.T. Wright notes that Jesus and the Apostle Paul seem to use the word "faith" with different emphases. When Jesus speaks of faith, faith means "recognizing that God is decisively at work to bring the kingdom through Jesus." This definition of faith emphasizes belief. For Paul, Wright suggests, the definition of faith includes the belief that Jesus is Lord and that God raised him from the dead, but it also includes the grateful human response to divine love: faith is not JUST belief; it is also response. Consider Paul's epistle to the Ephesians:

"For it is by grace you have been saved, through faith—and this not from yourselves, it is the gift of God—not by works, so that no one can boast. For we are God's handiwork, created in Christ Jesus to do good works, which God prepared in advance for us to do." (2:8-10)

In this passage, we see that faith is not simply a matter of belief but, if it is true faith, always entails a response in the form of good works. This idea is also important in the book of James, which insists that "faith without works is dead" (2:26); citing Abraham's obedience as an example; his faith was "made complete" by the action he took in accordance with his faith. (James 2:22)

Still, there is a certain tension between "faith and works;" Paul says, for example, that "in Christ Jesus neither circumcision nor uncircumcision has any value. The only thing that counts is faith expressing itself through love." (Galatians 5:6) It seems that while trusting in external markers (such as circumcision) does not, in itself, constitute faith, at the same time, faith demands expression "through love."

The Ephesians passage cited above also indicates something important and essential about Christian faith: Though it is human response, faith itself is a gift from God; it is God who enables a person to respond in faith.

Finally, the epistle of Hebrews gives a concise definition of faith: "Faith is confidence in what we hope for and assurance about what we do not see." (11:1) This definition demonstrates one of the things that makes faith a challenge—and underlines the need for God to grant faith as a gift: we do not yet see, for example, everything in the world put to right; with everything on earth as it is in heaven. And yet, faith enables us to hold onto our hope that this will one day be so. However, as some scholars have noted, the words "confidence" and "assurance" in Hebrews 11 have the connotation of words used in legal documents; "assurance," for example, is akin to a "title deed." Faith is our "title deed," in effect, to the things that we hope for and yet have not seen.

In Mere Christianity, C.S. Lewis wrote of faith as "the art of holding onto things your reason has accepted, in spite of your changing moods." This is one reason many churches collectively affirm the articles of their faith by reciting certain creeds; as the theologian Jaroslav Pelikan has said, the creeds help to remind Christians of the faith to which they've committed themselves, even if at a given moment in time, it is difficult to hold onto that faith.

Begin by reading aloud:

When people talk about religion, the word "faith" often comes up. In the Bible, faith is a very important word; a very important idea. But it is not always so simple to understand what people mean when they talk about Christian faith.

In the New Testament, the word for "faith" is somewhere between a noun and a verb, which means it is both an idea and an action. To have "faith" is not simply to believe that something is true. Having faith also means taking action on the thing that you believe to be true.

When the Apostle Paul writes about faith, "faith," for him, means believing that Jesus is Lord and that God raised him from the dead. It also means the part of that belief that makes a person respond to that truth. Faith isn't just belief; it is response to that belief.

In the book of Ephesians, the Apostle Paul writes:

> For it is by grace you have been saved, through faith—and this not from yourselves, it is the gift of God—not by works, so that no one can boast. For we are God's handiwork, created in Christ Jesus to do good works, which God prepared in advance for us to do. (2:8-10)

In this line we can see that faith itself is a gift from God—if we believe that Jesus is Lord and that God raised him from the dead and we respond by doing good works, we do so because God helps us to do so in the first place. Faith itself is a gift from God.

Another New Testament letter, Hebrews, defines faith this way: "Faith is confidence in what we hope for and assurance about what we do not see." (11:1) This shows us one reason why faith is a gift from God: it is hard to believe in what you don't yet see. In our world there are still so many things that go wrong. Everything is not as it should be. Everything is not as God would wish it to be. But by faith we go on believing that God will make all things right. By faith we go on doing the good works that God gives us to do.

But the way Hebrews defines faith also shows us that faith is more than just sort of hoping that something will happen. The words it uses, confidence and assurance, are serious words—words that hold inside themselves a very strong promise, like a legal document.

Faith means holding onto believing in Jesus, and continuing to live in a way that shows we believe in Jesus, even when things are difficult.

Lesson 35

Romans 8:24-25; Romans 15:13; 1 Peter 3:15; and Hebrews 11:1
Hope

What the Parent Should Know: "Hope" is another word that, like faith, is often thrown around in ways that make its meaning seem hollow and empty. "Hope for the best," people say, when there isn't really any good reason to hope for the best. The word hope, like the word faith, is often employed in this way as a sort of stand-in for "positive thinking."

But that vaguely positive idea is not at all what Christians mean when we speak of hope. When Christians speak of hope we mean something much more solid, grounded in the belief that Jesus has already conquered the worst enemy, death, and that in a future time, he will conquer death completely, and make all things new. And so hope is intimately related to faith. As John Calvin wrote, faith gives birth to hope, and then faith is, in turn, sustained by hope.

In some important ways, hope is central to Christianity. In Romans 15:13, Paul refers to God as the "God of hope," indicating that hope is a significant attribute of God's very identity: God is the God of hope.

The theologian Jürgen Moltmann wrote that "From first to last, Christianity . . . is hope, forward-looking and forward-moving, and therefore also revolutionizing and transforming the present." In the New Testament, Moltmann wrote, Christian hope is directed toward a future reality that is not yet visible—though we are offered a glimpse of that hope in Christ's resurrection.

Paul writes in Romans 8:24-25, "Hope that is seen is no hope at all. Who hopes for what they already have? But if we hope for what we do not yet have, we wait for it patiently." Hope, then, is intimately related to faith. Calvin wrote, "Hope is nothing else than the expectation of those things which faith has believed to have been truly promised by God." Elsewhere he put it more simply, saying that hope is perseverance in faith.

Put more simply, we might say that hope is expectant faith amidst unpromising surroundings. If all were as it should be, if we had nothing to expect, long for, and wait for, we would have no hope. And so, following Moltmann, C.S. Lewis, and others, we might say that our very dissatisfaction with "the way things are" presupposes that the way things are—death, pain, decay, and so forth—are not the way things are supposed to be.

Hope is the Christian virtue that answers to this human dissatisfaction. But it is not a virtue arising from the flesh alone. As Paul writes in Romans 15, the source of the Christian hope is the God of hope, who, Paul prays, will "fill you with all joy and peace as you trust in him" so that you may "overflow with hope by the power of the Holy Spirit."

Hope is an eschatological position—a view on the end of things—that is imparted by the Holy Spirit and rooted in Christ's resurrection.

Begin by reading aloud:

What does it mean to HOPE for something?

Often when we use the word HOPE, we use it in a way that suggests that we are uncertain about what is going to happen. "I HOPE that we will have chocolate cake tonight." "I HOPE she will get here on time." "I HOPE that tomorrow turns out to be a sunny day." In each of these examples, the person speaking is not sure of what will come: there may not be chocolate cake, she may not get here on time, and it may rain tomorrow.

But when the New Testament writers speak about hope, they mean something rather different. When Christians speak of hope, we are talking about Jesus' resurrection, and what it means for the future. Because Jesus has defeated death, and promises to defeat it completely and make everything new, Christians have hope that bad things in the world, even death, will one day be gotten rid of.

What this means is that even when things in the world seem awful, Christians can have hope, because God has promised to make all things new, and has already begun keeping that promise by raising Jesus from the dead.

Hope is a very important idea in the Christian faith. The Apostle Paul even calls God "the God of hope." One Christian writer said that Christianity is all about hope: Christians are always looking forward to the future time when everything will be as it should be and God will dwell with his people.

The difficulty, of course, is that we don't actually see the things we hope for. If we did see them, it wouldn't be hope. That is what the Apostle Paul writes: "Hope that is seen is no hope at all. Who hopes for what they already have?"

Hope goes along with faith. If faith is what we believe about God, hope is what we believe God will do. Hope lives where things don't seem to be going well at all. When all is well, we do not need to hope that they will be better.

It is not always easy to hold onto hope that God really will raise people from the dead and make all things new. Hope is sometimes hardest to come by when we need it most—when things aren't going well at all.

But the Apostle Paul tells us that hope doesn't come from us. It comes from the God of hope, who, Paul writes, can fill us "with all joy and peace as [we] trust in him," so that we may "overflow with hope by the power of the Holy Spirit." Hope comes from the Holy Spirit.

Hope is believing that God has already written the end of the story of humanity by raising Jesus from the dead. It is not about trying to make the best of a bad situation, or about trying to think positively. It is about knowing, even when things are going badly, that God has already taken care of the ending, and that, because of him, all shall be well.

Lesson 36

1 Corinthians 13:13; and 1 John 4:8-16

The Greatest of these is Love

What the Parent Should Know: In concluding the famous "love chapter," 1 Corinthians 13, the Apostle Paul declares love the greatest of the three theological virtues (faith, hope, and love.) Throughout the chapter, Paul has sought to demonstrate that eloquence, wisdom, prophecy, generosity, self-sacrifice, and even faith itself are nothing without love.

It seems important to note that what "love" means is not always clear. We do not "love" our family in the same way that we may "love" coffee, nor does God love us in the way that we love God. For the purposes of this discussion, "love" refers to self-giving, self-sacrificing care—charity, as the old translations have it—toward others that mirrors the self-giving love of God, shown most clearly in the sacrifice of Jesus.

Though Jesus' example of love would seem enough to establish the supremacy of love, we may still wonder why Paul calls love "the greatest" of the theological virtues. There are probably at least four main reasons.

First, as John Calvin noted in his commentary on 1 Corinthians, "Love extends its benefit to others." By contrast, "Everyone derives advantage from his own faith and hope." Love, therefore, may be thought of as superior to the other theological virtues because it moves outward from the individual toward others. "[Love] holds at present the first place in the preservation of the church," Calvin wrote.

Second—and this insight comes from Calvin as well—unlike love, faith and hope are not perpetual, but are, rather, necessary only for a time. In 2 Corinthians 5:7, Paul contrasts "faith" with "sight." In the day that we see God and dwell with God, we will no longer NEED faith as such, because we will see. Similarly—and as is probably clear from the preceding chapter—hope is no longer necessary when the object hoped for (in this case, the Kingdom of God) has been realized.

Third, Paul may regard love as the greatest of these because, as Jesus teaches—and as Paul also affirmed—the law and the prophets are summed up in love for God and neighbor. In Romans 13:8-10, Paul says that the person who loves his neighbor has fulfilled the law. This is similar to Jesus' declaration (in Matthew 22:36-39 and elsewhere in the Gospels) that to love God and to love one's neighbor constitute the two greatest commandments and the summation of the law and the prophets.

Fourth, and finally, love is paramount among the virtues because, as John the Evangelist wrote in 1 John 4, God is love. "The one who does not love does not know God, for God is love," he writes in verse 8. In verse 16, he writes, "God is love, and the one who abides in love abides in God."

Love is the "greatest of these" because not only is it self-giving, everlasting, and law-fulfilling, it is the virtue that most closely mirrors the essential character of God.

Begin by reading aloud:
"I love the dog!

"I love potato chips!"

"I love Legos!"

"I love my grandma!"

"I love God!"

What does it mean to *love* something or someone? If you love something—even if that thing is a dog or a kind of a snack or a toy—you delight in it; you are probably eager to spend time with the dog, to tell other people about how great your favorite snack is, and to care for and protect your Legos.

Loving God and loving, say, your grandma, are, in one way, not so different. If you hate having your picture taken, but you know that your grandma loves to have pictures of you, you might allow your picture to be taken (and maybe you'll even smile for the picture), because you love your grandma enough to give up something for her sake.

God loves us in an unselfish way. Some people say that God created the world out of love—not because he needed to, but because he wanted to love us and delight in us, the way you might love and delight in your dog or cat or Lego creations. In sending Jesus to save people from this world of pain and death, God showed his love very clearly: love that is God-like gives up something for the sake of another.

In his letter to the church at Corinth, the Apostle Paul tells us that love is more important than just about anything. It's more important than being wise and clever and well-spoken. Even if we are really generous and are willing to give up lots of things—but not out of love—it means nothing at all. Love, Paul says, is even more important than faith and hope, which are themselves really, really important.

Why is love so important—the "greatest" of the virtues?

Love is important because it is focused on others rather than on ourselves. Faith and hope are things that we have within ourselves, that benefit us, but they motivate us to love—and love moves outward from us to others. If we have faith and hope in God, we can be free to love other people because of the love that we have received from God.

Love is also important because, unlike faith and hope, love lasts forever. As we have already seen, faith and hope don't go on forever. We need faith because we do not yet dwell with God the way that we will one day dwell with him. We need faith because we do not yet see everything in this world made right, the way God wishes it to be. Hope is what keeps our faith going, even when things around us seem pretty bad. But we won't always need hope, either, because when everything in this world is made right, and everything on earth is as God wishes it to be, the thing we Christians have hoped for will have come true.

Yet even after hope and faith are no longer needed—because we have what we have been hoping for and because we see what we have had faith in without seeing—love will go on.

Love is also important because, as Jesus said, to love God and to love one another are the purpose of all the laws God ever gave. Love is the object, or goal, of all of God's teaching. Similarly, the Apostle Paul said that the person who loves his neighbor has already kept the law.

Finally, Jesus' beloved disciple, John, tells us several times that God IS love. If we do not love, he says, we do not know God. But if we do love—if we abide in love, which means dwelling in it, living in love—we abide in God.

Love is the "greatest" of faith, hope, and every other virtue because not only is it selfless and everlasting, it sums up what God desires from us—and it sums up who God really is.